EAT YOUR WAY TO LIFE AND HEALTH

ALSO BY JOSEPH PRINCE

For more information on these books and other
inspiring resources, visit JosephPrince.com.

JOSEPH PRINCE

EAT YOUR WAY TO LIFE AND HEALTH

UNLOCK THE POWER OF THE HOLY COMMUNION

EMANATE
BOOKS

Published in Nashville, Tennessee, by Emanate Books, an imprint of Thomas Nelson. Emanate Books and Thomas Nelson are registered trademarks of HarperCollins Christian Publishing, Inc.

Cover design by 22 Media Pte Ltd.
Cover copyright © 2019 by 22 Media Pte Ltd.
Illustrations copyright © 2019 by 22 Media Pte Ltd.

Thomas Nelson titles may be purchased in bulk for educational, business, fund-raising, or sales promotional use. For information, please e-mail SpecialMarkets@ThomasNelson.com.

Unless otherwise noted, Scripture quotations are taken from the New King James Version®. © 1982 by Thomas Nelson. Used by permission. All rights reserved.

Scripture quotations marked AMP are from the Amplified® Bible. Copyright © 1954, 1958, 1962, 1964, 1965, 1987 by The Lockman Foundation. Used by permission. (www.Lockman.org)

Scripture quotations marked NASB are from New American Standard Bible®. Copyright © 1960, 1962, 1963, 1968, 1971, 1972, 1973, 1975, 1977, 1995 by The Lockman Foundation. Used by permission. (www.Lockman.org)

Scripture quotations marked NIV are from the Holy Bible, New International Version®, NIV®. Copyright © 1973, 1978, 1984, 2011 by Biblica, Inc.® Used by permission of Zondervan. All rights reserved worldwide. www.Zondervan.com. The "NIV" and "New International Version" are trademarks registered in the United States Patent and Trademark Office by Biblica, Inc.®

Scripture quotations marked NLT are from the Holy Bible, New Living Translation. © 1996, 2004, 2007, 2013, 2015 by Tyndale House Foundation. Used by permission of Tyndale House Publishers, Inc., Carol Stream, Illinois 60188. All rights reserved.

Scripture quotations marked YLT are from Young's Literal Translation. Public domain.

All italics in Scripture quotations and testimonies were added by the author for emphasis.

ISBN 978-0-7852-2936-0 (eBook)
ISBN 978-0-7852-2927-8 (HC)
ISBN 978-0-7852-3130-1 (IE)
ISBN 978-1-4041-1245-2 (custom)

Library of Congress Control Number: 2019944304

Printed in the United States of America

19 20 PC/LSCH 10 9 8 7 6 5 4 3

CONTENTS

INTRODUCTION

Did you know you can ask God for a long, good, and healthy life?

Are you aware that God is still healing people today? And have you ever wondered if it is the will of God for you to be healed?

I don't know what circumstances you are confronted with as you hold this book in your hands. Perhaps you or your loved one has been diagnosed with a critical illness, and you are still reeling from shock, fear, and helplessness. Or maybe you have suffered a relapse of a condition you thought you had beaten, and you have resigned yourself to it being "God's will."

My friend, whatever situation you might be faced with, do not give up.

Not now.

Not ever.

No matter how dire your medical report might be, God can still turn your situation around. He is a God of miracles, and whatever giant you might be faced with today, He is bigger.

Your outward circumstances might be discouraging. You may be surrounded by intravenous drips, respiratory ventilators, or other medical equipment. The X-ray report you received, that lump the doctors found in your body, or that spreading patch on your skin may be foreboding. But you know what? You can *see* these things, and that means they are *temporal.* The Bible tells us that "the things which are seen are temporary, but the things which are not seen are eternal" (2 Cor. 4:18).

There is an enemy who uses the visible to snare you and oppress you with fear and discouragement. But I believe the Lord arranged for you to have this book in your hands because He wants you to keep your eyes on Him—the invisible God who is eternal. He will never leave you nor forsake you. And, even now, He is reaching out to you through the pages of this book. You have a God who loves you so much He gave His own life for you on the cross.

And yet people have somehow believed the lie that sometimes it is God's will for us to be sick. There are even those who claim that God uses sickness to "chastise" us or teach us a lesson. These lies have robbed His people of partaking of their blood-bought right to divine health. These lies have caused too many believers to simply accept sickness in their bodies.

My friend, God is *not* the author of sickness, disease, and death. The destructive power of disease and death was released through an act of eating when Adam and Eve ate from the Tree of Knowledge of Good and Evil. But God never intended for man to suffer disease and sickness. In fact, God never intended for man to die. Death came into the world because Adam sinned against God, and the wages of sin is death (Rom. 6:23).

The good news is, our beautiful Savior didn't just die for our sins—He also paid the price for the healing of our sicknesses and diseases with His own body. And because of His work on the cross, we can believe for healing and divine health. The Bible declares that "by His stripes we are healed" (Isa. 53:5).

How can we receive this provision of health and wholeness? Just as death and sickness came through the act of eating, I believe God has ordained that another act of eating reverses the curse brought about in the garden of Eden. I believe life, health, and healing can also be released through the simple act of eating.

In other words, *you can eat your way to life and health.*

What am I talking about? I am talking about the holy Communion.

The truths behind the holy Communion have been neglected by the body of Christ, with many seeing it as a mere ritual or tradition and partaking of it only a few times a year, or at most once a month. But because of the revelations God has unlocked for our church, we have been partaking of the holy Communion every Sunday for years. Many of our church members even partake of the Communion on a daily basis, with some partaking several times a day!

I have received healing testimonies from people all around the world since I started preaching the gospel of grace more than two decades ago, and especially when I started to preach on how God has ordained the holy Communion as a channel of receiving healing, health, and wholeness. As more and more people got hold of the teachings on the Lord's Supper, testimonies of healings began to stream in, and I cannot wait to share some of them with you in this book. Whether you are facing a medical challenge or you simply desire to live in a greater measure of health, I know you will be blessed by the truths in this book.

Interestingly, many people think the way to live a long and healthy life is to watch what they eat. That's why so many fad diets have come and gone, and we are constantly told we need "health foods" like barley greens, coconut oil, and spirulina, just to name a few, in order to stay healthy. I was stunned to discover that the dieting industry in America alone is a seventy-billion-dollar industry today,[1] with businesses trying to push all kinds of dieting methods, supplements, and plans.

Don't get me wrong. By all means eat well, choose the right foods, and stay away from excesses that will damage your body. But our dependence cannot be on diets, fancy activity trackers, exercise apps, and health foods. Thank God for nutritionists and fitness instructors. They are fighting the same battle. Our trust, however, has to be in the redemption purchased by Christ and not in creation. I will elaborate on this in the following chapters.

Divine health and long life can only come from God. Unlike the health foods, diet, or vitamins and supplements industries trying to sell their products, God's provision for life and health is not sold in a bottle, nor is it a plan or a pill. It has been given to us freely, but it came at an astronomically high price that was paid on the cross of Calvary by the Son of God Himself.

I wrote this book because I want you to receive—through partaking of the holy Communion—the full benefits of all the Lord Jesus has purchased for you on the cross. I want you to know beyond the shadow of a doubt that God wants you healed, whole, and well. I want you to know that God's heart is for you to enjoy a long, healthy, and satisfying life.

Here are just some of the questions I hope to answer for you in this book:

- Is it God's will to heal me?
- Do I qualify for His healing power?
- What should I do if I am sick?
- Is God punishing me with sickness and disease?
- Of what relevance is the holy Communion to me?
- Can God heal my loved ones?
- How can I have a long, healthy life?
- What should I do when I don't see results?

In answering these questions, I don't want to share my personal opinions with you. I want to show you everlasting promises from the Word of God. I want to share testimonies from Scripture as well as from people who have received healing even though doctors had told them their conditions were terminal or incurable.

What God has done for them, He can do for you too.

My friend, your healing breakthrough is on its way, and I can't wait for you to receive every iota of the blessings our Lord Jesus paid for you to enjoy. Let me show you how you can eat your way to life and health.

1.

COME TO THE TABLE

This book you are holding is not an ordinary book.

I feel strongly that I am on assignment from God, an assignment to bring us to a place where every child of God can walk in divine health all the days of his or her life!

I fully believe the Lord has given me a mission to teach on the health-giving, life-imparting, healing power of the holy Communion, and I cannot wait to tell you more.

This is not a new revelation or some passing fad. I have been preaching, teaching, and practicing the insights the Lord has given me for close to two decades now. We have a congregation of more than thirty-three thousand people meeting across multiple services in multiple locations every Sunday. Every Sunday, at every service, including our kids' services, we partake of the holy Communion together as a church.

The holy Communion is not just something for me to teach. I am fully convinced of its efficacy, and I personally partake of the Lord's Supper on a daily basis. There are seasons when I even partake of it several times a day, and I can't begin to tell you how the freedom to freely receive the Lord's Supper has blessed me and my family.

GET A POWERFUL REVELATION
OF THE COMMUNION

I have preached many messages on the holy Communion during the last twenty years. But I preached what I consider to be a milestone message on April 7, 2002, titled "Health and Wholeness Through the Holy Communion." It wasn't just another sermon. The truths unveiled that day led to the healing and transformation of umpteen lives around the world and released a flood tide of revelations that continue to reverberate through many lives.

My friend, I don't want *you* to miss out on that message! Would you allow me to take you back in time? I have prepared a link to the message as my gift to you. You can listen to it by going to JosephPrince.com/eat. As you listen, I want you to know this: God is not limited by time or space. You will be listening to a word the Lord put in my heart *for you* many years ago. It was powerful then, but I believe it has never been more relevant than right now.

THE REVELATION OF THE HOLY COMMUNION HAS NEVER BEEN MORE RELEVANT THAN RIGHT NOW.

Whether this is the first time you are hearing me teach about the holy Communion or the hundredth time, I pray that your life will be revolutionized as the Lord reveals His truths to you. Whatever sickness or pain you might be dealing with, may your healing begin today as you learn more and more about how you can partake of Jesus' finished work through the holy Communion.

The fruits of teaching the holy Communion have been astounding. Since I started preaching on it, healing testimonies have been pouring in from around the world. If you are one of those who have written to me, thank you. From the bottom of my heart, *thank you*. I am so humbled you would take the time to share your testimony with me. I may not be able to respond to everyone or to share every testimony during my preaching, but reading about what the Lord has done for you and your loved ones has blessed me beyond measure, and I want you to know the word of your testimony has also gone on to help others to overcome the enemy in their lives (Rev. 12:11).

In particular, I want to say a special thank you to those of you who have sent me copies of your medical reports, scans, X-rays, and other medical documentation that validate the Lord's healing in your lives. I rejoice to know you are walking in the health our Lord Jesus paid for you to enjoy. I rejoice even more to know you have experienced His love for you in such a tangible way.

HEALTH IS THE GREATEST BLESSING

Would you agree that apart from the gift of salvation—receiving Jesus as our Lord and being saved from eternal destruction—the greatest blessing we could receive is health? You can have a wonderful family, but if you are flat on your back and cannot enjoy being with them, that would be misery. As for money, you might be able to afford the latest medical treatment or best surgeons, but all the money in the world cannot buy health.

I have no doubt God wants you and me to enjoy His blessing of health. When Jesus walked on earth, He didn't walk on water or calm storms all the time, but He *healed* all the time. Every village He stepped into, everywhere He went, He went about doing good and healing all who were oppressed (Acts 10:38).

WE HAVE BEEN ROBBED!

One of the reasons I am so passionate about teaching on the holy Communion is that I was a victim of flawed, legalistic teaching that kept me in fear and bondage for many years when I was a young

Christian. I wouldn't be surprised if some of you reading this were taught the same things.

I was taught to "examine myself" before coming to the Lord's Table and warned not to partake of the holy Communion if there was sin in my life that made me unworthy. I was told that if I did, I would bring judgment on myself. I would become weak and sickly, and I might even die before my time. As a result, I was so fearful of the Communion I never partook of it.

JESUS DIDN'T WALK ON WATER OR CALM STORMS ALL THE TIME, BUT HE *HEALED* ALL THE TIME.

After all, I was no fool. Why would I want to risk it? I wasn't living in sin or anything like that, but what if there was some sin in my life I didn't know about or had forgotten to confess? To make matters worse, I was told I could commit not just sins of commission (things I did), but also sins of omission (things I failed to do), and even sins of transmission (sins committed by my ancestors). How could I ever know if I was "worthy" enough?

In the previous church I attended, I remember how those who wished to partake of the holy Communion were invited to go forward, and we would have to walk to the altar in front of the church. I was a youth leader then, so I would pretend to go forward together with those who were receiving the Communion. After standing for some time, I would go back to my seat and make it appear as if I had already received the Communion. But I never partook of it.

Why? Because of fear.

I was robbed of my inheritance because of well-meaning but erroneous preaching that put an invisible fence around something that was meant to be a *source* of health and healing and a blessing for God's people. A fence was put around it saying, "Don't come near unless you are worthy." I don't want you to be robbed like I was, and that is why I want you to see for yourself what the Word of God says. Are you ready?

MISINTERPRETATION OF SCRIPTURE
LEADS TO WRONG BELIEFS

How did such wrong beliefs come about? They stem from a misinterpretation of the apostle Paul's teaching on the holy Communion in his letter to the Corinthian church:

> Therefore whoever eats this bread or drinks this cup of the Lord in an unworthy manner will be guilty of the body and blood of the Lord. But let a man examine himself, and so let him eat of the bread and drink of the cup. *For he who eats and drinks in an unworthy manner eats and drinks judgment to himself, not discerning the Lord's body. For this reason many are weak and sick among you, and many sleep.* (1 Cor. 11:27–30)

Somehow, people have misunderstood verses 27 and 29 and have taught that we cannot partake of the Communion if we are "unworthy" because of our sins. But Jesus' blood has already been shed for us, and as believers, we are the righteousness of God in Christ (2 Cor. 5:21). We are completely righteous and worthy not because we are perfect, but because *He* is perfect.

Now I want to make it clear that I am *against* sin. But we don't have to be perfect to come to the Lord's Table. If that were a prerequisite, *no one* would be able to partake! You might not think you have committed any serious or major sins, but to God, sin is sin, and if you fail in even one area, you are counted guilty of all (James 2:10). Thank God that even when we fail, we have "redemption through His blood, the forgiveness of sins, according to the riches of His grace" (Eph. 1:7).

WE DON'T HAVE TO BE PERFECT TO COME TO THE LORD'S TABLE.

I also want to point out that verses 27 and 29 do not say that those who are *unworthy* cannot partake of the Communion. Look closely.

Paul was talking about the *manner* in which one partakes of the Communion. The apostle was writing to the Corinthian church, which was treating the Lord's Supper with irreverence, eating to satisfy their hunger with no consideration for others and even getting drunk. Paul described the manner in which they were partaking:

> So when you meet together, it is not to eat the Lord's Supper, for when you eat, each one hurries to get his own supper first [not waiting for others or the poor]. So one goes hungry while another gets drunk. What! Do you not have houses in which to eat and drink? Or do you show contempt for the church of God and humiliate those [impoverished believers] who have nothing? (1 Cor. 11:20–22 AMP)

It is clear Paul was correcting them for treating the Lord's Supper like any other meal, rather than partaking of it in a *manner* that was worthy of what our Lord Jesus had ordained it to be. They were treating the Communion as something ordinary instead of seeing it as holy and set apart.

For us today, to partake of the Communion in an unworthy manner is to be like the Corinthian church, treating the elements of the Communion as *common, insignificant,* and *powerless.* It is to treat the Communion elements as natural and ordinary and to fail to recognize the potent, sacred force we get to hold in our hands. It is to disdain the elements and to be like the children of Israel, who got so familiar with the manna God in His grace provided that they saw the bread from heaven as worthless (Num. 21:5). It is to simply go through the motions of eating the bread and taking the cup without valuing the significance and power they contain.

DON'T SIMPLY GO THROUGH THE MOTIONS OF PARTAKING OF THE BREAD AND THE CUP WITHOUT VALUING THEIR SIGNIFICANCE AND POWER.

Maybe you have never really understood why Christians partake of the Communion, and you have only been partaking because you were told to. It is an empty ritual to you, something your church organizes once a month, or only on special occasions like Good Friday. Maybe you are partaking of the Communion superstitiously—you are giving it a go simply because you have heard healing testimonies from others, and you are hoping it might work its "magic" for you too. Or maybe you see it as a sentimental custom or quaint tradition that simply reminds Christians about the roots of their faith. Maybe when you hold the elements, all you see is a cracker and some juice, nothing more.

If that sounds like you, may I tell you that *you* have also been robbed? The Bible says God's people are destroyed "for lack of knowledge" (Hos. 4:6). Your lack of knowledge about what the holy Communion is really about has been destroying you, and you don't even know it!

WE HAVE THE REAL FOUNTAIN OF YOUTH

Let me tell you why I preach so strongly about the holy Communion, and why I partake of it every single day. Let me tell you why the holy Communion is ingrained as part of the DNA of our church and why I believe it is more powerful than any medicine, any medical procedure, any antibiotic, and any chemotherapy used to heal our bodies. Let me tell you why I believe the holy Communion is the proverbial "fountain of youth" mankind has been in search of for generations and why I believe every time we partake of it, we are causing our youth to be renewed like the eagle's (Ps. 103:5).

> EVERY TIME WE PARTAKE OF THE COMMUNION, OUR YOUTH IS BEING RENEWED LIKE THE EAGLE'S.

The earth has been under a divine judgment ever since Adam sinned. Aging, disease, and death are all part of this divine sentence. The reality is, we live in a fallen world and these effects of the divine sentence are happening to *all* our mortal bodies. But God *never* intended for His children to suffer any of it. That is why He sent His Son to bear our sins and sicknesses on the cross. That is why He provided the holy Communion as a way to escape the divine judgment that is on this world, to offset its effects. The holy Communion is a supernatural channel for His health and wholeness to flow into our bodies. While the world is getting weaker and sicker, I believe we are getting stronger and healthier each time we partake of the Communion by faith!

THE HOLY COMMUNION IS A SUPERNATURAL CHANNEL FOR HIS HEALTH TO FLOW INTO OUR BODIES.

There are some who have misconstrued 1 Corinthians 11:27 to say that when we are unworthy and we partake of the Communion, God will judge us by giving us sicknesses. It makes me sad that people would inadvertently accuse our loving Father of inflicting us with sickness, when He made the ultimate sacrifice to *take away* sicknesses from us. Isn't it just like the deceiver to erect fences of wrong beliefs around the very channel the Lord meant as the antidote to sickness and disease? Isn't it just like the enemy to put up these fences so God's people would be too fearful to partake of His provision?

The early church clearly understood how powerful the Communion is. That's why they didn't partake of it only once in a while. The Bible tells us they broke bread "from house to house" (Acts 2:46). When they met on Sunday, the main reason wasn't to hear preaching and teaching. I want you to see this for yourself:

> Now on the first day of the week . . . the disciples came together *to break bread.* (Acts 20:7)

Even though the apostle Paul was the guest speaker that weekend, the main reason they gathered was to break bread. If people today only knew the magnitude of the power contained within the Lord's Supper, they would be like the early church, partaking of the Lord's Supper as often as they could and receiving as much of His benefits as they could. We have been robbed, people! It's time to wake up!

Let us always examine ourselves, not for sins (as they have been washed away by the blood of Jesus), but to ensure we partake in a manner *worthy* of the Lord's Supper, with a revelation of His finished work. Let us always be conscious that, as we partake of the bread, we are partaking of Jesus' body that was broken so ours might be whole (1 Cor. 11:24; Isa. 53:5). And as we partake of the cup, let us be conscious we are receiving His blood that was shed for the forgiveness and remission of *all* our sins (Matt. 26:28; Col. 2:13).

> **PARTAKE OF THE LORD'S SUPPER WITH A REVELATION OF HIS FINISHED WORK.**

HE IS WITH YOU IN THE MIDST OF YOUR TRIAL

But if God wants us to be healthy, and Jesus' body was broken for us, why are there Christians who are sick? I personally know believers who are battling severe illnesses, and I am sure you do too. You or your loved one might even be facing a health challenge right now.

If you are fighting a medical condition, please know that it is okay for you to have doubts and questions. The Lord knows the confusion and pain you feel, and He wants you to know He is with you through it all. I know it can be hard to keep trusting Him when you are going through a fiery trial. But keep trusting Him, my friend. He *is*, right now, your very *present* help (Ps. 46:1). Keep fixing your eyes on Him. He is faithful, and He will never leave you nor forsake you (Deut. 31:6).

Daniel 3 records the story of three friends (Shadrach, Meshach, and Abed-Nego), who were bound and thrown into a fiery furnace when they refused to bow to and worship the gold image set up by King

Nebuchadnezzar. The furnace was so hot that the men who threw them in were killed by the heat. But the king saw the three friends walking in the midst of the fire, and he saw a fourth man with them who was "like the Son of God" (Dan. 3:25). Amazed, the king called them out, and he and all his officials saw that the fire had had no power over them. Not a single hair on them was singed, their clothes were not scorched or damaged, and there was not even the smell of smoke on them. As a result, the king acknowledged that there was no other God who could deliver like their God, and the three friends were not only released, they were also promoted.

> **YOU WILL EMERGE FROM YOUR TRIAL SO MUCH STRONGER THAN BEFORE YOU WENT IN.**

Beloved, your Lord Jesus has promised that "*nothing* shall by any means hurt you" (Luke 10:19). Even if you are going through a trial, He will deliver you. Just as He was in the fire with Daniel's three friends, He is *with you*. I pray in Jesus' name you will emerge from this trial so much stronger than before you went in. I declare that this disease shall have *no* power over you, and that the Lord will deliver you so completely you will come out of this without even the smell of smoke on you!

HOW TO ESCAPE BEING WEAK AND SICK

I want to share with you something that I believe can help us to experience more of His healing power. The apostle Paul draws our attention to the reason many Christians are weak, sick, and even dying prematurely. Aren't you glad he used the word *reason* and not *reasons*? I am not saying every believer's sickness is due to this. I am just pointing out that in His Word, God highlights this as the reason many Christians are weak, sick, and asleep (dead prematurely). This is good news because it means that when we know what this reason is, we can avoid it.

For he who eats and drinks in an unworthy manner eats and drinks judgment to himself, *not discerning the Lord's body. For this reason many are weak and sick among you, and many sleep.* (1 Cor. 11:29–30)

The "reason" highlighted by Paul is "not discerning the Lord's body." The word *discerning* is translated from the Greek word *diakrino*, which means "to make a distinction."[1] (If you want to know more about the key Greek words used and their meanings in 1 Corinthians 11:28–32, please refer to the appendix.) There are some who recognize that Jesus' blood was shed for the forgiveness of our sins, but they don't recognize that His body was broken so that our bodies can be well. There are also those who lump both the bread and cup as one, seeing both as representing the forgiveness of sins instead of separating the two.

But Jesus didn't just suffer and die for our forgiveness. He also died for our healing. The psalmist David wrote, "Bless the LORD, O my soul, and forget not all His benefits: Who forgives all your iniquities, who heals all your diseases" (Ps. 103:2–3). The same Jesus who purchased the forgiveness of *all* our sins also removed *all* our diseases. The failure to make a distinction and see that the Lord's body was broken for our diseases to be healed causes many to be sick and weak.

If many are sick and weak because they have failed to discern the Lord's body, then it stands to reason the opposite is true: those who *discern* that His body was broken for our health will be healthy and strong, and will live long, good lives! That, my friend, is why I am writing this book. There is such healing power in the holy Communion, but too many people have been robbed of this gift either because they do not know about it or because they have been taught wrongly about what the Lord meant for it to be.

Every time we partake of the Lord's body, we are ingesting health, vitality, strength, and long

> THE SAME JESUS WHO PURCHASED THE FORGIVENESS OF *ALL* OUR SINS ALSO REMOVED *ALL* OUR DISEASES.

life. If there is disease in the body, the disease will be supernaturally driven out. If there is decay and degeneration, the deterioration will be reversed. If there is pain, it will be removed. The results may not be spectacular and immediate, but they are sure and will surely come. And I pray you will experience them for yourself.

CANCER DISAPPEARED AFTER PARTAKING OF THE COMMUNION

Some years ago, doctors found a huge tumor in my uncle's throat. A biopsy showed it was cancerous. He was then sent for another more detailed scan, and the pathologist told him the cancer was aggressively spreading all over his neck and behind his tongue. My uncle told me that the moment he heard what the pathologist said, he gave up hope he would live. But before he went for his surgery to try to remove the tumor, his daughters, who had been attending our church for years, went to him and said, "Let's have Communion together, Dad. Let's pray and believe God."

He shared that as they partook of the Communion, he felt hope rising in his heart for the first time, and he partook believing that Jesus was his healer and believing that the body of Jesus would make a difference in his body right there in the hospital ward. After that, he went for the surgery and the doctors removed the mass from his throat. The amazing thing is, when they did a biopsy on the growth that was taken out, they found absolutely no trace of cancer in the tumor, and his doctors could not explain it!

> EVERY TIME WE PARTAKE OF THE LORD'S BODY, WE ARE INGESTING HEALTH, VITALITY, STRENGTH, AND LONG LIFE.

Multiple scans before the surgery had confirmed that the growth in his throat was cancerous. In fact, the tests showed that the cancer was spreading and that it was aggressive. And yet, when the tumor was removed, there was no trace of cancer in it. Somehow the Lord had caused the cancer to supernaturally disappear, and I believe it happened when my uncle and his family partook of the Communion.

In the same way, if there is a condition in your body, and your doctors have given you a negative prognosis, do not fear. We may not know how our healing can take place, but let's have faith in the finished work of Jesus. "With God, all things are possible" (Matt. 19:26).

Even though we just started talking about the holy Communion, I pray that this chapter has already helped to answer some of your questions and that you are now excited to receive its benefits freely. You are so loved. Don't live as though you don't have a Savior. Whatever condition you might have been diagnosed with, do not despair. He has paid the price for you to be well. And He has made it easy for you to receive not just His love and forgiveness, but His healing power as well.

I want to invite you to the Lord's Table. The table has been prepared, not by human hands that can falter and fail, but by the perfect One whose hands were nailed to the cross for you. *He* prepares this table in the presence of your enemies, and invites you to come to partake of His body broken for you and His blood shed for you. Come boldly to the table and partake by faith and receive your healing.

> HE HAS MADE IT EASY FOR YOU TO RECEIVE BOTH HIS FORGIVENESS AND HEALING POWER.

If you have received Jesus as your Lord and Savior, you have been made worthy by the blood of the Lamb. You have been washed clean of all your sins. Don't allow the enemy to rob you any longer. Partake of the Lord's Supper with thanksgiving, knowing that each time you partake, you are getting healthier, stronger, and younger in Christ!

2.

NOT ANOTHER DIET PLAN

You may have picked up this book thinking I am advocating some kind of new dieting plan. The reality is, I am! But the food and drink I am talking about are not natural food and drink. And they have nothing to do with the amount of carbohydrates you are allowed to eat or whether or not they are from an organic source. In this chapter, I want to talk to you more about this *supernatural* food and drink and the key to living a long, healthy life *God's way*.

WHAT IS YOUR HEALTH BASED ON?

According to the Centers for Disease Control and Prevention, from 2015 to 2016, 70 percent of adults in the United States aged twenty and over were overweight or obese.[1] That's a pretty startling statistic, if you ask me. What is of even greater concern is that obesity is linked to rising rates of dozens of chronic illnesses and conditions including diabetes, heart disease, cancer, depression, and even infertility.[2]

Maybe you are wondering how you can ensure you live a long, healthy life. May I tell you chasing the latest dieting fad or buying the most updated activity tracker is not the answer? While some diet plans can produce results like weight loss, many people regain their weight with a vengeance once they stop their diets. As for activity trackers, I remember being at an electronics store and having a chat with the owner when the trend first started. He shared with me how there was such a demand for activity trackers that they quite literally flew off his shelves. But a study showed that while one in ten Americans over eighteen years old owned an activity tracker, more than half of those said they had stopped using it altogether.[3]

Please hear me out. I am not saying you should not eat well or exercise. Of course you should! I am just pointing out that while billions of dollars are being poured into the dieting and weight loss markets each year, the results they yield are mixed and often temporary. I am all for fitness plans or devices that can help people achieve their health goals. I personally observe a healthy diet, and I also exercise and go for walks on a regular basis.

But may I submit to you that as believers, we should not be obsessed with or dependent on diets and fitness regimes for our health? God has something special set aside for His children, and that's the gift of His divine health. It is a *supernatural* health that is not based on the food we eat or how hard we hit the gym. If all that could lead to divine health and life, then anyone, including nonbelievers, would be able to walk in it!

> **GOD HAS SOMETHING SPECIAL SET ASIDE FOR HIS CHILDREN—THE GIFT OF SUPERNATURAL HEALTH.**

THE ONLY GUARANTEE TO DIVINE HEALTH

Many believers are pursuing food and diet as their key to health, and there are many books on what to eat and what not to eat. For instance, there are believers who are advocating going back to the diet Adam and Eve would have eaten in the garden of Eden. This means eating more fruits, grains, and seeds, as though we could go back to the time before Adam sinned. But we cannot pretend the fall never happened—it did!

There are also those who advocate the Mediterranean diet that our Lord Jesus would have eaten. I agree a Mediterranean diet is good, but if you think about it, every single person Jesus healed *was* on the Mediterranean diet, and they still fell sick. Other diets have also come and gone, with proponents championing different things, from having no carbohydrates, to intermittent fasting, to vegan foods. Unfortunately, eating right doesn't guarantee good health. A person can eat only what is considered by nutritionists as the best organic superfoods and be phenomenally disciplined with their daily exercise routine, yet still fall terminally ill and have their life shortened by sickness. Why is that? Creation is fallen. The answer is not found in *creation*; it is found in *redemption*!

I am not knocking special kinds of diets. If you have been on such diets and they have been good for you, praise the Lord! I am just saying our trust and dependence cannot be in the foods we eat to make us healthy or to give us long lives. There is no hope in creation. Whether it is adhering to certain diets, making use of herbal remedies, or eating organic foods, they all come from this created world. They can be beneficial, but they cannot guarantee health because the earth is fallen.

THE ANSWER IS NOT FOUND IN *CREATION*; IT IS FOUND IN *REDEMPTION*!

All of creation is groaning and subject to death and decay (Rom. 8:21–22 NLT). The Bible even tells us, "For it is good that the heart be established by grace, not with foods which have not profited those who have been occupied with them" (Heb. 13:9). The only sure thing we should establish our hearts on is *grace*, and grace is the very person

of our Lord Jesus. The only guarantee is the finished work of our Lord
Jesus Christ.

PUT YOUR TRUST IN REDEMPTION, NOT CREATION

As long as we are depending on our eating and exercising to keep us
healthy instead of trusting in the Lord, our dependence is still on creation (natural means) and not on redemption (His supernatural work).
Even as we eat healthily and exercise regularly, if we want to walk in
supernatural health, then our trust should be in
a supernatural God and the supernatural food
He has given us.

> TO CREATE, GOD ONLY HAD TO SPEAK; TO REDEEM US, HE HAD TO *BLEED*.

Man has tons of research devoted to creation and entire libraries and research centers
focused on studying questions such as how
the earth was formed and how life began. But
do you know what God thinks of creation? He
spent just one chapter in the whole Bible talking
about creation.

When it comes to redemption, however, God spent more than ten
chapters in Exodus alone talking about the blood sacrifices, offerings,
and tabernacle of Moses because they all speak of the glories and beau-
ties of His Son and the work of redemption He was sent to carry out.

For God to create, He only had to speak. But for God to redeem us,
He had to *bleed*. Redemption cost God so much more than we could ever
imagine. If we think we can look to creation to make us healthy, do you
know what we are saying? If we could achieve the blessing of health by
our discipline and good works, then we are saying the cross was useless
and Jesus' sufferings were in vain. But, my friend, that is not so. There
is no hope in creation; there is only hope in the cross!

THE FOOD THAT BRINGS
HEALTH AND WHOLENESS

Let me tell you more about this supernatural food and drink we get to take. It is the only food and drink that is not based on fallen creation or dependent on the efforts of fallen man. When we eat and drink this supernatural food, we are partaking of the work of redemption and not creation.

Our Lord Jesus said, "I am the living bread which came down from heaven. If anyone *eats of this bread*, he will live forever; and the bread that I shall give is *My flesh*, which I shall give for the life of the world" (John 6:51). The word *life* here is the Greek word *zoe*, which is the same Greek word used in the Septuagint when God breathed into Adam and Adam received life (Gen. 2:7). While *zoe* refers to the life that God lives by, *zoe* also refers to physical life, health, vitality, and wholeness.[4] The food that God has given us to eat is not perishable food but *living* bread—Jesus, who came from heaven and was given for us to have life.

> **THE FOOD WE HAVE IS NOT PERISHABLE BUT *LIVING* BREAD, GIVEN FOR US TO HAVE ABUNDANT LIFE.**

If you are wondering how Jesus can give us His flesh to eat, you are in good company, because the Jews who heard what Jesus said asked the same question (John 6:52).

There are some who think Jesus was simply talking about believing in Him. But I want to draw your attention to how our Lord Jesus went on to say, "For My flesh is food indeed, and My blood is drink indeed. He who *eats* My flesh and drinks My blood abides in Me, and I in him" (John 6:55–56).

Did you know two different Greek words are used here for the word *eats*? When Jesus said, "If anyone *eats* of this bread, he will live forever" (John 6:51), the generic Greek word *phago* for *eats* was used. *Phago* can be used in a physical sense or in a spiritual sense, as in to feed on Christ.[5] But when Jesus said, "He who *eats* My flesh and drinks My blood abides in Me, and I in him" (v. 56), the Greek word used for *eats* is *trogo*, which means "to gnaw or crunch,"[6] like when eating nuts.

There is no way you can spiritualize a crunching sound. Jesus was not talking about spiritually eating or feeding here. He was talking about physically eating, about chewing with a crunching sound!

To understand more what our Lord was referring to, look at what He said on the very night He was betrayed, when He knew He would lay down His life for us:

> And as they were eating, Jesus took bread, blessed and broke it, and gave it to the disciples and said, "Take, eat; this is My body." Then He took the cup, and gave thanks, and gave it to them, saying, "Drink from it, all of you. For this is My blood of the new covenant, which is shed for many for the remission of sins." (Matt. 26:26–28)

What was our Lord Jesus talking about when He broke the bread and gave it to His disciples, saying, "Take, eat; this is My body"? And what was He referring to when He gave them the cup, saying, "This is My blood of the new covenant, which is shed for many for the remission of sins"? Yes, He was talking about His crucifixion, but He was also instituting the holy Communion, a physical meal.

The Communion is God's ordained way or delivery system for us to receive the unending, holy, youthful, overcoming, and perpetually healthy life Jesus has as we "eat His flesh and drink His blood." The Bible tells us that the "whole multitude sought to touch Him, for power went out from Him and healed them all" (Luke 6:19). Our Lord Jesus' body emanated such divine health, power, and life that simply touching even the hem of His garment caused many to be healed (Mark 6:56). Can you imagine the power we are ingesting when we partake of the bread and cup—His broken body and shed blood?

SEEING JESUS IN THE MATZAH BREAD

The bread our Lord Jesus would have used when He broke bread on the night of the Passover and said, "Take, eat; this is My body which is broken for you" (1 Cor. 11:24) was unleavened Jewish matzah bread. Matzah bread is a flat, cracker-like bread specially prepared for the Passover. I wanted to highlight this because today most of us think of soft, fluffy loaves when we mention bread. But this is not the kind of bread Jesus was talking about.

When our church was smaller, we purchased matzah bread and broke it into pieces for our congregation when we partook of the holy Communion together each week. As we ate the bread, we could hear crunching sounds from the people around us, and I believe we were hearing the scripture in John 6:56 being fulfilled—hearing what it sounds like to *trogo*!

Jewish leaders who didn't even believe in Jesus have passed down through the centuries the instructions for making the matzah bread. If you look at the picture of the matzah bread below, you will notice it is striped, pierced, and burnt.

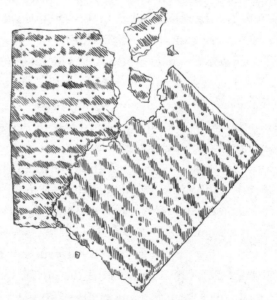

The matzah bread is a practical, visual reminder
of what Jesus suffered for our healing.

Do you know why the matzah bread is made this way? I believe the Lord ordained it to be striped, pierced, and burnt so that each time you partake of the holy Communion, you are reminded afresh what Jesus went through for you:

- *Striped*—because it is by the stripes He bore when the soldiers scourged Him that we are healed (Isa. 53:5).
- *Pierced*—because His hands and feet were pierced by the nails, His side was pierced by the soldier's spear (John 19:34), and His brow was pierced by the crown of thorns (John 19:2).
- *Burnt*—because the fire of God's judgment fell upon Him when He carried our sins (Isa. 53:4).

HE WAS BEATEN AND CRUSHED FOR YOU

Why did our Lord Jesus choose the bread and wine as the elements He wanted us to partake of "in remembrance" of Him (1 Cor. 11:24–25)?

I believe it is because they are practical and visual reminders of what happened to Him as He went to the cross. Both grain and grapes have to go through a process of being pulverized before you can get bread or wine.

You don't get wine from just eating grapes. The grapes have to first be trampled upon and completely crushed. They are then left in the dark to ferment. That's what happened to our Lord Jesus.

It is important we discern the Lord's body for our health. Each time you partake of His broken body by eating the bread, don't rush through it. Partake with a revelation of what He did for you, and meditate on the process the bread had to go through. To get bread in Jesus' time, the wheat stalks first had to be threshed. This could have been done through beating (Judg. 6:11 NASB) or with the use of a threshing sledge (Isa. 41:15). Whatever the process, it was a violent one that involved beating, crushing, and cutting the wheat to separate the grain from the stalks. But that wasn't all. To get flour, the grain had to be ground in a millstone or beaten in a mortar. After that, water had to be added and the flour was then kneaded and punched into dough before it was baked over fire.

All this is a picture of what happened to our Lord Jesus. To become the Bread of Life for you and me, He was brutally beaten and pounded over and over again. It started in the Garden of Gethsemane, when a great multitude with swords and clubs came to arrest Him (Mark 14:43). He was then bound and brought to the high priest's house, where He was condemned by the high priest and Sanhedrin. They mocked Him, spat on Him, and beat Him. They blindfolded Him and struck Him on His face (Luke 22:63–64; Mark 14:65).

> **EACH TIME YOU PARTAKE OF HIS BROKEN BODY, DO IT WITH A REVELATION OF WHAT HE DID FOR YOU.**

He was then sent to Pontius Pilate, who had Him savagely scourged by Roman soldiers (Matt. 27:26). The movie *The Passion of the Christ* tries to depict the sufferings our Lord Jesus went through. The movie was criticized because people felt the scourging scene was too violent, but the truth is, it didn't even come close. The Bible tells us "His visage was marred more than any man, and His form more than the sons of men" (Isa. 52:14). He was so badly mutilated He did not even look like a man anymore, and I believe the people who were present had to look away and hide their faces because they could not bear to look at His grotesque, quivering form (Isa. 53:3).

But His ordeal did not stop there. A whole garrison of soldiers then gathered around Him and put a scarlet robe on His battered body. They twisted a crown of thorns and rammed it on His head. They put a staff in His right hand, bowed before Him, and mocked Him. They spat on Him and took the staff and struck Him on the head again and again, driving the thorns deeper and deeper into His flesh with each blow. They were bent on completely humiliating Him. When "they were finally tired of mocking Him," they stripped Him of the robe and put His own clothes on Him again. Then they led Him away to be crucified (Matt. 27:27–31 NLT).

We can never fully imagine or understand the horrifying torture, degrading humiliation, and excruciating pain our Savior endured for our sakes. But did you know He had the power to stop His ordeal and overcome His tormentors at any point? When the troops came to arrest Him, they said, "We seek Jesus of Nazareth." The Bible tells us He stepped forward and spoke the awesome name of God that was revealed to Moses—I AM (Ex. 3:14)—and the soldiers drew back and fell to the ground (John 18:5–6). That's power. But He *chose* to lay down His life and endure all the pain—for your healing and my healing. That's love!

Our Savior didn't want you to be saved from just your sins. If that was all He wanted to accomplish, the shedding of His perfect, atoning blood alone would have been enough. In the Old Testament, when the children of Israel brought their sacrificial animals to the priests as atonement for their sins, the animals never suffered. They were killed humanely using a method known today as *shechita* to ensure they died swiftly and painlessly.[7]

But our Lord Jesus didn't die a quick, painless death. He suffered like no other, going through hour after hour of unimaginable torture before He finally died. Look at this scripture:

> [Christ] Himself bore our sins in His own body on the tree, that we, having died to sins, might live for righteousness—by whose stripes you were healed. (1 Peter 2:24)

T. J. McCrossan, a Greek scholar, highlighted that in the original Greek text, 1 Peter 2:24 actually says, "by whose stripe you were healed." He explained that the word *stripe* was in the singular and not plural form, because Jesus was scourged till there was not even one sliver of skin left on His back. His back was one bloody stripe, one big gaping laceration.[8] According to some accounts, scourging could be so brutal that even the internal organs of the victims could be seen.[9]

My friend, He loves you so much. He went through all that torture because a punishment was required for your well-being and health, and He allowed the punishment to fall upon Himself (Isa. 53:5 AMP). Just by reading this and knowing what He did for you, I believe healing has begun in your body. Whatever disease you might have been diagnosed with, Jesus bore it on His own body so you would not have to suffer it.

He endured it all. The unimaginable pain, the utter degradation. And the Bible tells us why: it was "for the joy that was set before Him" (Heb. 12:2).

> WHATEVER DISEASE YOU MIGHT BE DIAGNOSED WITH, JESUS BORE IT ON HIS OWN BODY SO YOU WOULD NOT HAVE TO SUFFER IT.

The joy? What was the joy set before Him that gave Him such strength to endure the cross?

It was His love for you! It was the joy of seeing you well, of seeing you set free from pancreatic cancer, set free from leukemia, set free from rheumatoid arthritis, set free from Lou Gehrig's disease. Whatever condition you might have, Jesus has taken it all.

If you are sick right now, and maybe you are reading this from your hospital bed, say this: "Thank You, Lord Jesus, You went through all that *for me*."

THE SIMPLE ACT OF EATING CAN REVERSE THE CURSE

Maybe you are thinking to yourself, *How can something as simple as eating the holy Communion lead to my healing? I find that hard to believe!* Let me ask you this: How did sin come into the world? How did death, sickness, disease, and pain come into the world?

It was through the simple act of *eating*.

God never meant for man to grow old and to have sickness. God never meant for man to die. It was Adam's sin of eating from the Tree of Knowledge of Good and Evil that brought forth death. The Bible tells us that "through one man sin entered the world, and death through sin, and thus death spread to all men, because all sinned" (Rom. 5:12). Adam's one act of eating caused the fall of man and all the curses that accompanied the fall. His one act of eating gave the world a one-way ticket to suffering, depression, disease, and death.

God hated the sin that was destroying man. In His great love for you and me, God sent His own Son. Our Lord Jesus disrobed Himself of His deity and became a man so He could bear all our sins upon His own body. And at the cross, God unleashed His holy judgment not upon you and me, but upon the body of Jesus.

Because of the cross, we can come boldly to God, knowing *all* our sins are forgiven. Because of the cross, we can have full assurance sickness and disease have *no right* to be in our bodies, for our Lord Jesus has already borne every sickness on His body! Our Lord Jesus reversed every curse by His death on another tree. Today we can receive all that Jesus did on the cross by partaking of the holy Communion—through the simple act of eating.

> SICKNESS AND DISEASE HAVE *NO RIGHT* TO BE IN OUR BODIES, FOR OUR LORD JESUS HAS ALREADY BORNE EVERY SICKNESS ON HIS BODY!

DON'T UNDERESTIMATE THE ACT OF EATING

Unfortunately, it is the very simplicity of the holy Communion that makes it so hard for many people to believe it can be effective. All they can see is a small piece of bread and a little cup of juice. They cannot imagine how something so seemingly insignificant can drive out disease or cause them to live a long life. After all, it wasn't manufactured after years of meticulous research by scientists in a laboratory filled with cutting-edge technology.

I am not against medicine. If your doctor has prescribed medicines for you, please continue to take them. But even as you take them or undergo treatment, your trust can be in your Lord Jesus to heal you. Partake of the holy Communion together with your medication. Medicines are man-made and come with warnings listing all their possible side effects. But the holy Communion was provided by God Himself, and the only side effects are that you will get younger and stronger each time you partake of it!

GOD USES WEAK THINGS TO CONFOUND THE MIGHTY

When we dismiss the Communion elements because they appear so insignificant and weak, we are forgetting the way God works. The Bible says, "God has chosen the weak things of the world to put to shame the things which are mighty" (1 Cor. 1:27). Time and again, we see how God defeated the enemies of the children of Israel not through military might but through seemingly insignificant things.

EVEN AS YOU UNDERGO MEDICAL TREATMENT, TRUST IN YOUR LORD JESUS TO HEAL YOU.

God used a sling and a stone in the hand of a young shepherd boy to bring down Goliath, the mighty champion of the Philistine army (1 Sam. 17:38–51). He used a hammer and a tent peg in the hands of a defenseless woman to destroy Sisera, the ruthless Canaanite military commander who had oppressed the children of Israel for twenty years (Judg. 4:3–22). He used the jawbone of a donkey in the hand of Samson—a single man—to slay a thousand Philistines (Judg. 15:15–16).

In the same way, when you hold the elements of the Communion in your hands, they may appear small and inconsequential. Your flesh may try to tell you, "This is silly. What can this little cracker do?" or "There's no point getting your hopes up. Nothing can help you." But don't listen to those lies. Don't make the mistake of despising the bread and the cup, because God can use what seems so small to utterly destroy diseases the world has no cure for.

When a Gentile woman came to the Lord Jesus seeking healing for her severely demonized daughter, He referred to healing as "the children's bread." Do you know what the woman said to Him? "Yes, Lord, yet even the little dogs eat the crumbs which fall from their masters' table." Jesus then said to her, "O woman, great is your faith! Let it be to you as you desire." And that very hour, her daughter was healed (Matt. 15:22–28).

> **GOD CAN USE WHAT SEEMS SO SMALL TO UTTERLY DESTROY DISEASES THE WORLD HAS NO CURE FOR.**

What do you think the children's bread that is laid on the "masters' table" is a shadow of? The holy Communion! You and I sit at the Master's table because we are sons and daughters of the Most High God, and we partake freely of the Lord's Supper. If even the "crumbs" that fell from the table could heal the woman's child, how much more healing and life we shall receive when we have the substance of the holy Communion!

SUPERNATURAL RECOVERY FROM STROKE

Since we are talking about how we can eat our way to life and health, I want to share a testimony from Zach, someone in Singapore who exercises almost daily and who in his own words is "careful with his diet":

One day while I was getting ready for work, I suddenly lost strength in my left leg and arm. I couldn't put on my trousers and leaned against the cupboard as I slid to the floor. I shouted for my wife and told her I felt unwell.

I started to pray in the Spirit, calling out to Jesus. My wife also prayed and declared that by Jesus' stripes, I am healed!

About five minutes later, strength came back to both my leg and arm. I could stand up and proceeded to walk to the sofa and sat down. Although the strength in my leg and arm returned, I felt my motor skills had not.

My family took me to the hospital where I underwent some tests. The MRI scan showed I'd suffered a mild stroke. My world sank totally. I found myself questioning, *How can this be? I exercise almost daily and I'm careful with my diet.*

I was admitted to the hospital and above the door of my room hung a cross. I looked to the cross and claimed the finished work of Christ, pronounced my body healthy because of His perfect work, and kept claiming the finished work of Christ.

We also *partook of the holy Communion as a family*, and I anointed myself with oil. I prayed and claimed God's promises in Psalm 23:4–6.

By the next day, I could feel that my strength and motor skills had returned. When the doctor came to examine me in the morning, he confirmed that my strength had returned to around 80 to 85 percent and sent me for physiotherapy. On the third morning, the doctor examined me and informed me I could be discharged as I had regained 95 percent of my strength.

In my follow-up review, I was given the all clear to go back to my regular exercise routine. Soon after that, I competed in an 18K run and finished it in just over two hours.

I thank God for my fast recovery and thank you, Pastor Prince, for your teachings on partaking of the holy Communion and applying the anointing oil for healing, and for your grace messages week in and week out.

I give Jesus all the praise! Amen.

Zach suffered a stroke and had the terrifying experience of suddenly losing strength in half of his body. A stroke can lead to permanent damage in the body, but praise the Lord, Zach recovered very quickly, and I fully believe it was because of the Lord's protection and healing.

But what I want you to see is this: Zach was perplexed that he could suffer a stroke since he exercised almost daily and was careful with his diet. At the end of the day, Zach's dependence could not be on his eating and exercising. He could only look to the cross and depend on the finished work of Christ. And that's our only surety as well! Did you notice how Zach declared that his body was healthy because of Jesus' perfect work (and not because of his disciplined lifestyle)?

If you find yourself facing a medical condition, may I encourage you to do what Zach did? I rejoice with Zach for his quick recovery, but no matter how dire your prognosis continues to be, keep standing on the finished work of Christ. Keep speaking His Word over yourself and keep thanking the Lord for His promises. Read for yourself the promises Zach held on to after he suffered a stroke:

> Yea, though I walk through the valley of the shadow of death,
> I will fear no evil;
> For You are with me;
> Your rod and Your staff, they comfort me.
> You prepare a table before me in the presence of my enemies;
> You anoint my head with oil;
> My cup runs over.
> Surely goodness and mercy shall follow me
> All the days of my life. (Ps. 23:4–6)

Know that even if you are walking through a dark valley and the shadow of death looms over you, you do not have to fear, for the Lord is *with you.*

See the Lord preparing a table before you in the presence of your enemies. Notice that the Lord prepares a table before you *in the presence* (not in the absence) of your enemies. The apostle Paul referred to the holy Communion as "the Lord's table" (1 Cor. 10:21). That means even when the symptoms are in your body, and even when the pain is there, the Lord wants you to come to His table and eat. Eat of all that our Lord Jesus has done for you on the cross by partaking of the holy Communion. His body was broken so that yours might be whole.

DO NOT FEAR, FOR THE LORD IS WITH YOU.

It is human nature to feast and celebrate only *after* we see that our problems have been solved and our enemies eradicated. But that's not what God wants you to do. He loves you so much, and right now He says to you, "Rest. Sit down. Eat. For I will fight your battle. I will defeat your enemies!" With each bite when you eat, see yourself getting supernaturally stronger. See the tumor shriveling up. See His health flowing into your body.

Don't be afraid of your enemies. They might be all around you, but you can eat from the Lord's Table with joy, knowing that *surely*, goodness and mercy and His unfailing love follow after you all the days of your life! If you look up the Hebrew word for *follow* in Psalm 23:6, you will see that it is *radaph*, and *radaph* means "to chase, hunt, or pursue."[10] See your Daddy God's goodness and love chasing you down wherever you go. Even if you have to undergo surgery, chemotherapy, or an organ transplant, He is right there with you. In the operating theater, He is there. In the intensive care unit, He is there. Do not fear—He is with you, and your enemies have *no power* over you!

3.

NONE FEEBLE, NONE SICK

I believe that as you delve more into understanding the healing power of the holy Communion, your faith to receive all the Lord has for you is enlarging. As your revelation grows, faith follows. Faith is not a struggle. The more you see Jesus, the more you will have faith. Right now, I pray that your vision of Jesus and all He has done for you at the cross will be further enlarged as I unveil to you some beautiful and powerful truths from the Passover meal that I know will strengthen your faith to receive your healing. You may be amazed to discover that the Passover meal the children of Israel ate in Egypt foreshadowed our eating of the holy Communion today—and they both point to the finished work at the cross!

REMEMBERING THE FIRST PASSOVER

When I was in Israel with some of my pastors several years ago, I was invited by a dear friend to join his family as they celebrated the Jewish Passover. They are Messianic believers completely transformed by the gospel of grace, and it was a great privilege for my pastors and me to partake of the Passover meal with them. The fact that we were in Israel made it even more special for me, and I treasured the intimate time we had as a family of believers.

During that Passover meal, what stood out distinctively to me was the question the children at the table asked the elders: "Why is this night different from all other nights?" They were following an oral tradition of the Jewish people, passed down from generation to generation. More importantly, this question set up the opportunity for the elders to share with the next generation how the Lord had delivered the children of Israel from slavery and bondage.

THE MORE YOU SEE JESUS, THE MORE YOU WILL HAVE FAITH.

The elders told the children about all the judgments against Egypt their forefathers had witnessed, from the frogs that came up from every river, pond, and stream to cover the land of Egypt, to the dust that became lice and infested the Egyptians, and the clouds of locusts that ravaged the land, devouring all its crops. You can imagine the gasps of wonder and looks of utter amazement on the children's faces as they heard of the Lord's rescue plan to deliver His people when Pharaoh repeatedly refused to free them (Ex. 7—11).

Then the elders told the children about how the Lord had instructed the Israelites to select a lamb without blemish for each household. The *body* of the lamb was to be roasted and eaten with unleavened bread and bitter herbs, while its *blood* was to be applied on the lintel and two doorposts of their houses (Ex. 12:22). I have asked my team to prepare the picture below that shows how the Israelites would have applied the blood. Can you see how applying the blood as instructed would have formed a picture of the cross?

Applying the lamb's blood on the lintel and two doorposts (top illustration)
would have formed a picture of the cross (bottom illustration).

The elders narrated how the angel of death went throughout Egypt at midnight, and the cries from their Egyptian oppressors were heard throughout the land as every firstborn son—even the mighty Pharaoh's—was struck dead.

The children heard how, while this happened, their ancestors huddled together in their homes. Some were excited and expectant, knowing this was the night they would finally be freed from years of crushing slavery, while others were terrified the destroyer would also strike their homes. But whatever their state of mind was, death *passed over* their houses as long as the blood of the lamb was on their doorposts and lintels. On that same night, Pharaoh finally let go of his stubborn grip on the children of Israel, and they began their exodus from the land of Egypt. They were free.

SHADOW VERSUS SUBSTANCE

Every year, Jews around the world continue to reenact how the Lord rescued them so powerfully during the night of the first Passover by partaking of a carefully prepared meal and observing certain traditions. But you know what? The Passover was only a *picture* of what our Lord Jesus was going to accomplish at the cross when He delivered mankind from slavery to a greater pharaoh—Satan himself!

What the children of Israel had was just the shadow. What we have under the new covenant inaugurated by His shed blood is the *substance*. It was not by coincidence our Lord Jesus instituted the holy Communion on the same night He celebrated the Passover (Matt. 26:17–29; Mark 14:12–25; Luke 22:7–20). The apostle Paul referred to Him as "Christ, our Passover Lamb" (1 Cor. 5:7 NLT) because His sacrifice on the cross was the fulfillment and fullness of the Passover the children of Israel had been celebrating for generations.

"WHY IS THIS NIGHT DIFFERENT FROM ALL OTHER NIGHTS?"

I mentioned earlier that during the Passover celebrations each year, the children ask their elders, "Why is this night different from all other nights?"

When you partake of the holy Communion, ask yourself the same question: *Why is this night different from all other nights?*

It might not be nighttime when you are partaking of the holy Communion, but as you partake, you are remembering what happened when our Lord Jesus was nailed to the cross, suspended between heaven and earth, and rejected by man and by God. When Jesus was born, midnight became midday as angels filled the sky and the glory of God shone all around (Luke 2:8–11). But as Jesus hung on the cross for you and me, midday became midnight as darkness covered the land (Matt. 27:45). Even if you are going through a dark period, take heart. Your Savior went through the darkness so you can always stand in His wonderful light (1 Peter 2:9) and see the Sun of Righteousness arise with healing in His wings (Mal. 4:2).

Because of what happened that day on the cross, you can trust God for freedom from the disease that has shackled you. You can freely receive the blessings of abundant life, health, and strength. You can rest in the knowledge you have been marked and covered by the blood of His protection and no plague can come near your dwelling. You can have the confidence that the same God who freed a whole nation from oppression fights *for you*. And if God is for you, no sickness, no virus, and no medical condition can prevail against you (Rom. 8:31)!

> IN YOUR DARK SITUATION, SEE THE SUN OF RIGHTEOUSNESS ARISE WITH HEALING IN HIS WINGS.

HEALED THROUGH PARTAKING OF THE LAMB

Do you know what happened when the children of Israel ate the Passover lamb? God liberated the Israelites from severe oppression and freed them from their captivity. But that wasn't all. He also "brought them out with silver and gold, and *there was none feeble among His tribes*" (Ps. 105:37).

Exodus 12:37 records that about six hundred thousand men left Egypt on the night of the exodus. But when you include the women and children, scholars estimate about two to three million Israelites were freed that night.[1]

Out of these, none—not a single one—came out feeble!

Not one sick, not one who stumbled, not one who lacked strength or had mobility problems despite years of harsh and severe labor they had to endure under their slave masters (Ex. 1:13–14 AMP). Contrary to some cinematic interpretations of the exodus, no one was carried out on a stretcher or limped slowly out of Egypt. My Bible says there were *none feeble*!

By the way, you don't have to be sick to enjoy the benefits of the Communion. Even if there is nothing wrong with you, you can believe for a greater measure of health. Whether you are partaking of the Communion for healing in your body or you are simply believing for new strength, I want you to see that you can believe for supernatural health like the children of Israel who partook of the Passover lamb. Those who were sick came out healed. Those who were weak came out strong. And those who were strong came out even stronger!

SUPERNATURAL HEALTH IMPARTED DURING PASSOVER

I want you to think about the backbreaking work the Israelites were forced to do and the beatings and whippings they suffered, not to mention malnutrition from the poor diet they probably had to scrape together and the abject living conditions they must have faced.

Do you think that in the natural, every single one in this nation of slaves could have been completely strong and healthy? Of course not. And among so many of them, I am sure there would have been elderly slaves as well. So how is it possible the Bible records that "none were feeble"?

I submit to you that something happened to their bodies on the night of the Passover as they ate the roasted lamb.

I believe many among them *were* weak and sickly before the night of the Passover. But *something happened* that reversed all the effects of repetitive stress injuries, muscle and ligament strains, incapacitating work injuries, age-related conditions, and infectious diseases that could have plagued the Israelites because of the conditions they lived under. *Something happened* that night that caused them to supernaturally become healthy. The children of Israel were filled with divine strength for the journey ahead that God knew would be long, and I believe their youth was renewed like the eagle's (Ps. 103:5; Isa. 40:31).

If that could happen for the children of Israel when all they had was a natural lamb (the shadow of the true Lamb of God that you and I have), *how much more* should we see our bodies healed, our strength rejuvenated, and every weakness reversed when we partake of the holy Communion? We have the *true* Lamb of God, the *substance* and the *reality* of the shadow the Israelites believed in. *How much more* should we have none feeble and none sick among us!

You may not have physical chains binding you today nor whips from brutal slave masters driving you. But maybe you are no stranger to a chronic condition that has bound you for years. Perhaps you have been tormented by recurring symptoms that have left you in constant pain. As you partake of the holy Communion, see yourself partaking of Jesus, the true Passover Lamb. Even if you don't see immediate results, keep partaking. As you partake, know your freedom is at hand. As you partake, know that you are getting stronger and healthier.

> YOUR FREEDOM IS AT HAND. AS YOU PARTAKE, YOU ARE GETTING STRONGER AND HEALTHIER.

BACK HEALED IMMEDIATELY UPON RECEIVING COMMUNION

Dalene, a lady from Pennsylvania, experienced the healing power of the true Lamb of God as she partook of the holy Communion. I pray that you will be encouraged as you read her testimony:

On Wednesday at work, my back became very painful and I felt nauseous. I went home and slept the rest of the afternoon and through the night until late next morning.

I awoke and my back was still painful so I watched your video on the holy Communion. My faith was built up to believe the oppression and pain were already borne in the body of Jesus.

As I partook of the Communion, I saw Jesus giving me the bread, telling me, "This is My body." I ate and visualized the transformation in my body as I received His healing. I reflected that if a roasted lamb could strengthen and energize Israel, how much more would the Lamb of God heal a daughter of God. My back was immediately healed, the oppression lifted, and I was restored. Glory to God!

The grace message has transformed my life in virtually every area. Thank you so much for preaching His message.

Praise the Lord!

By the way, may I draw your attention to how Dalene was watching a video that taught about the holy Communion *before* she herself partook? If you are trusting God for healing, I want to encourage you to do what Dalene did, to listen to teaching on the holy Communion before you partake. As you listen or watch, may your faith be built up to receive *all* the Lord has done for you, and may you also experience healing and freedom from oppression.

FORGIVEN, MADE RIGHTEOUS, AND PROTECTED BY HIS BLOOD

Before the Passover, God said to the children of Israel, "And *when I see the blood*, I will pass over you; and the plague shall not be on you to destroy you when I strike the land of Egypt" (Ex. 12:13).

You might be feeling anxious because doctors have detected some abnormalities in your recent health check. Or perhaps a few of your relatives have succumbed to a particular disease and you are fearful you might be next.

My friend, I want you to know *you do not have to be afraid.*

Among the children of Israel, those who were quaking in their homes when the angel of death passed through the land were fearing needlessly. They could have spared themselves the tears and trepidation not just because their anxiety did not do anything for them, but because the lamb's blood was already on their doorposts. They were saved from destruction not because they were Israelites and not because of their good behavior or anything they did. They were saved just because of one thing—the blood of the lamb. In the same way, *you* have been saved by the blood of the Lamb. If you are a believer, you can put your trust and confidence in the blood on the doorposts of your life. Rest in the Lamb!

What's more, the Lamb who died for you at Calvary was not an ordinary lamb. It was the true Lamb of God, who takes away the sin of the world (John 1:29). The blood that was shed for you was not the blood of a natural lamb, but the royal blood that flows through Immanuel's veins. The cross transcends time, and on that day His blood washed you clean of *every* sin—past, present, and future. You are completely forgiven not because of your good deeds but because of His blood (Eph. 1:7).

Stop disqualifying yourself from His healing because of the failures in your life. Stop believing the enemy's lies that you don't deserve to be healed because of the mistakes you have made or because you have not been going to church enough. When God looks at you, He doesn't see you in your failures and frailties. He only sees His Son because you are *in Christ*. Because you are in Christ, you are completely accepted in the Beloved (Eph. 1:6), and you are *already* blessed with every spiritual blessing (Eph. 1:3). This means that even if there are symptoms in your body, God sees you as healed. Each time you partake of the holy Communion, start seeing yourself the way God sees you. See yourself healed, whole, and filled with divine strength and life.

Each time you take up the cup of the new covenant in His blood

(1 Cor. 11:25), know that the blood of Jesus "speaks better things" under the new covenant than the blood of Abel (Heb. 12:24). Abel's blood had cried out for vengeance (Gen. 4:10). Jesus' blood cries out for your redemption (Eph. 1:7; 1 Peter 1:18–19), your justification (Rom. 5:9), your victory over the enemy (Rev. 12:11), and so much more!

JESUS' BLOOD CRIES OUT FOR YOUR VICTORY OVER THE ENEMY.

Because of Jesus' blood, God imputed righteousness to you the moment you accepted Jesus as your Lord and Savior. There is no barrier between you and God (Eph. 2:13). You can come before God boldly. You can draw near to Him to find help in your time of need (Heb. 4:16; 10:19–22). Whatever challenges you might be facing, whether it is your health, emotions, finances, or relationships, you don't have to handle them alone. The Creator of all heaven and earth calls you His own precious child (John 1:12; 1 John 3:1). Run to Him!

And if the blood of an animal could protect the children of Israel from the plague, *how much more* will the holy, sinless blood of the Son of God protect you from destruction and shield you from any sickness? I am not saying that as a believer you will never fall sick. Unfortunately, we live in a fallen world. But if you do fall sick, you have the blood-bought right to declare that by the stripes your Savior bore, you are healed. You have the blood-bought right to claim health and wholeness as your portion.

HOW TO PARTAKE OF THE LAMB

Don't you love seeing Jesus in the Passover? I really believe the more you see Him in the Passover, the more you will experience healing and deliverance. Don't just skim through the book of Exodus and see it as a historical record of something that happened a few thousand years ago. I love the little details the Holy Spirit recorded, and I believe when you take time to search out the Scriptures, the eyes of your understanding will be opened and you will see revelations of Jesus you had never seen before.

For instance, look at God's instructions on *how* the Israelites were to eat the Passover lamb:

> Then they shall eat the flesh on that night; roasted in fire, with unleavened bread and with bitter herbs they shall eat it. Do not eat it raw, nor boiled at all with water, but roasted in fire—its head with its legs and its entrails. (Ex. 12:8–9)

The children of Israel were told *not* to eat the Passover lamb *raw*.

How does this apply to us? When we partake of the holy Communion, we should not be focusing on our Lord Jesus' life in raw form before He had been "burned" by the fire of God's judgment on the cross. We should not be seeing Him as a baby in a manger or as He is recorded in the Gospels *before* the cross. Neither should you see Jesus as simply being a moral leader or great teacher.

Yes, He is the most excellent expositor of the Scriptures, for He is the author of the Scriptures. But He is not just a teacher; He is God incarnate. He is Immanuel, God with us. And yes, He lived a perfect life, but it wasn't His perfect life that saved us. It was His sacrifice and death on the cross. In other words, we need to see Him "roasted in fire." That's what we need to meditate on when we partake of the Communion.

> **YOU HAVE THE BLOOD-BOUGHT RIGHT TO CLAIM HEALTH AND WHOLENESS AS YOUR PORTION.**

SEE HOW JESUS SUFFERED ON YOUR BEHALF

The children of Israel were also told not to eat the lamb "boiled at all with water" (Ex. 12:9).

I believe this means we should not water down or sanitize what Jesus did for us at the cross. Many traditional movies and paintings of Jesus on the cross depict Him looking very clean, with small wounds and only a few drops of blood.

But that is not what happened to our Lord Jesus at all, and such images are whitewashing what He went through for you and me. Because of the scourging and beatings He endured, the Bible says that at the cross Jesus' visage, or face, was beyond recognition. His form was marred more than that of any man (Isa. 52:14), to the point there was no beauty in Him (Isa. 53:2).

MEDITATE ON HIS SACRIFICE AND DEATH ON THE CROSS WHEN YOU PARTAKE OF THE COMMUNION.

No movie can ever portray how Jesus really looked on the cross. No one can even fathom it. Whenever you partake of the holy Communion, picture Jesus on the cross and remember how He suffered for your forgiveness and healing. Remember how He was marred and disfigured so you could be glorious in every way.

JESUS BORE THE FIRE OF GOD'S JUDGMENT

God also told the children of Israel to eat the lamb "roasted in fire." That's a picture of the fire of God's judgment on Christ. The next time you partake of the Communion, the next time you hold the bread in your hand, see His body burnt and smitten with our diseases on the cross, and see God unleashing His holy vengeance and righteous anger against our sins in the body of His Son. Sin had to be punished, and Jesus took it all on Himself so you and I need not bear the punishment.

On the cross, Jesus did not just *take* our sins; He *became* sin so we might become the righteousness of God in Him (2 Cor. 5:21). He also took our infirmities and bore our sicknesses on His own body

(Isa. 53:4 YLT; Matt. 8:17). Every tumor, every cancerous growth, every deformity, every rheumatoid arthritis, every kind of disease, He took upon Himself at the cross.

And as Jesus hung on the cross, He cried, "I thirst!" (John 19:28). Do you know why He was thirsty? Because the fire of God's holy vengeance and righteous indignation fell upon Him. He came under the judgment of God so you and I will *never* come under God's judgment (Rom. 5:9–11 NLT). Because our sins have been punished in the body of our substitute, it would be unrighteous for God to punish the same sins twice. Today God's holiness and God's righteousness are on our side, demanding our justification, demanding our forgiveness, demanding our healing, and demanding our deliverance.

> **JESUS CAME UNDER GOD'S JUDGMENT SO THAT AS BELIEVERS, YOU AND I WILL NEVER HAVE TO.**

PARTAKE EXPECTING PHYSICAL DELIVERANCE

I also love it that God told the children of Israel to partake of the Passover lamb in this manner:

> And thus you shall eat it: with a belt on your waist, your sandals on your feet, and your staff in your hand. (Ex. 12:11)

Why did they have to eat with belts on their waists, sandals on their feet, and staffs in their hands? God was telling them to be *ready* for their *physical* deliverance even as they ate the roasted lamb.

In the same way, when we partake of the Lord's Supper, let's partake with faith and expectancy. Let's partake expecting our miracle to take place, expecting our deliverance. That's what the Israelites did, and they came out with not one sick, not one feeble. I want to see that happening for my church and for all of you. We may not yet have come to the place where we can say there are "none feeble," but I believe we are on our way.

Even if you have a medical condition or pain in your body, partake of the Lord's Supper by faith, giving thanks that you are *already* healed, expecting to see the full manifestation of your healing. I believe each time we partake of the Lord's Supper, we are getting healthier and healthier, stronger and stronger!

GET READY FOR A NEW BEGINNING

If you are thinking to yourself, *I tried partaking of the holy Communion before but it did not work*, I have a word for you.

> **AS YOU PARTAKE OF THE LORD'S SUPPER BY FAITH, EXPECT TO SEE THE FULL MANIFESTATION OF YOUR HEALING.**

There is an enemy who wants to keep you enslaved to that medical condition in your life. The enemy wants to keep you in a place of despair and to keep you so focused on your disappointments you cannot lay hold of God's promises for you. That is what he did to the children of Israel. When Moses told the Israelites that God would rescue them from their bondage, the Bible tells us "they refused to listen" as they had "become too discouraged by the brutality of their slavery" (Ex. 6:6–9 NLT).

But you know the story. God did not abandon them even though they refused to listen. He knew they were in a state of despair because they had suffered under the yoke of slavery for so long. Do you want to know what the children of Israel did that caused God to rescue them so mightily? I want you to read this for yourself:

> Then the children of Israel groaned because of the bondage, and they cried out; and their cry came up to God because of the bondage. So

God heard their groaning, and God remembered His covenant with
Abraham, with Isaac, and with Jacob. (Ex. 2:23–24)

The children of Israel were so oppressed all they could do was groan.
There was nothing left in them to compose any prayers. And the Bible
tells us *God heard their groaning* and He remembered His covenant with
Abraham, Isaac, and Jacob.

I am sharing this with you because I want you to know that you *do
not* need to craft impressive declarations of faith or do anything for God
before He hears you. Just a groan will reach the throne. A simple sigh
from you will reach the throne room of your Abba in heaven. If just a
groan from the children of Israel could activate the covenant God had
cut with their forefathers, how much more would your cry accomplish,
oh child of the Most High!

Maybe that condition in your body has shackled you for so long you
have told yourself to stop hoping, because if you don't get your hopes up,
at least you won't be disappointed again. Maybe you think you are not
qualified to pray because you just don't have "enough faith." You may
have heard that you have to pray without doubt in your heart (Mark
11:23), but you can't help but feel fear as you are confronted with the
size of the tumor, or how far the disease has spread, or the level of your
platelet count.

So you have simply stopped praying. Stopped
hoping. Stopped believing.

If any of what I have said seems all too familiar to
you, may I invite you to give the Lord another chance?

When God taught the Israelites to keep the first
Passover, He said, "This month shall be your beginning
of months" (Ex. 12:2). This speaks of a new beginning.

Perhaps you never had a revelation of how the
Lord Jesus suffered to pay for your healing. Perhaps you never knew
what power was contained in the holy Communion. But I pray that as
you continue to read this book, the eyes of your understanding will be

> JUST A
> GROAN WILL
> REACH THE
> THRONE.

opened to the exceeding greatness of His power toward you, and you will know that the same power that raised Christ from the dead works for you (Eph. 1:18–20).

Today I want to encourage you to take a step of faith. Let this day be your beginning of days. When you put your trust in the Lamb who was slain for you, you are stepping into a new beginning. Forget the former things. Forget the failures and disappointments of the past.

> **THE SAME POWER THAT RAISED CHRIST FROM THE DEAD WORKS FOR YOU.**

I want to invite you to once again start putting your faith in the One who gave His life for you. Take up the bread and say, "Thank You, Lord Jesus. You gave Your body to be broken so mine might be whole. By the stripes that fell on Your back, I see my body healed from the crown of my head to the soles of my feet."

Take the cup in your hand and say, "Lord Jesus, thank You for Your precious blood that has washed me clean from every sin. Today I partake of every inheritance of the righteous, which includes protection, healing, wholeness, and provision."

As you come to the Lord's Table, trust that you will experience what the Israelites did after partaking of the roasted lamb and coming out with not one feeble and not one sick. My friend, I am believing with you for your breakthrough. The enemy wants to keep you bound, but the Lord wants to set you free!

FOR YOU, NOT AGAINST YOU

I have shared with you some truths that I pray are burning in your heart right now. But maybe you are wondering if the disease you are fighting is somehow from God. Maybe you think He is punishing you for something you did and that there is a lesson He wants you to learn.

If you have believed any of the lies above, then you have fallen prey to Satan, who is the great deceiver and father of lies (Rev. 12:9; John 8:44 NLT). His *modus operandi* is to deceive you, and his master strategy is to convince you sickness is actually from God. I want you to know in no uncertain terms that your heavenly Father loves you, and He wants you well. He does not want your life to be cut short by sickness, and it is *never* His plan for you or your loved ones to suffer any sickness or disease.

> IT IS *NEVER* HIS PLAN FOR YOU OR YOUR LOVED ONES TO SUFFER ANY SICKNESS OR DISEASE.

GOD IS NOT OUT TO DESTROY YOU

I want you to be very clear on this: there is an enemy who wants to destroy you. Our Lord Jesus said, "The thief does not come except to steal, and to kill, and to destroy" (John 10:10). Satan is a murderer (John 8:44) and a thief who is out to steal from you. When Satan deceived Adam and Eve in the garden of Eden, sin came into the world. But man did not just lose his position of righteousness. We also lost our relationship with God and confidence in His heart for us. Fear and condemnation entered, robbing us of our faith and our trust in a good God.

And just as Satan stole from Adam and Eve, he wants to steal from you your health, your youth, and your joy. He wants to destroy every dream you have cherished and rip you from the embrace of the people in your life. He wants to kill you because he knows there is a call and purpose on your life that only you can fulfill, and he wants to find every way to snuff you out.

Every time you find yourself or your loved ones being robbed, be it of health, finances, or family relationships, God is *never* behind it. Man was created to enjoy everything God has provided, and that includes health. Our Lord Jesus said:

> "I have come that they may have life, and that they may have it more abundantly." (John 10:10)

Can you see His heart for you? The thief comes to steal, kill, and destroy, but our Lord Jesus came to *give* you life and not just life but "life more abundantly"! When Jesus said this, He wasn't simply referring to biological life. The Greek word used for *life* here is *zoe*, and it refers to the highest form of life, the life God lives by.[1] He does not want you to simply keep breathing. He wants so much more for you, and He came to give you a quality of life God Himself possesses, a life that is beyond ordinary human life.

JESUS CAME TO GIVE YOU NOT JUST LIFE BUT LIFE MORE ABUNDANTLY!

If you have been told you will die young or don't have long to live, I want you to know you don't have to accept the diagnosis. Thank God for doctors who have dedicated their lives to alleviating pain and suffering, but with all due respect, doctors don't have the final word in our lives—the almighty God does.

He is the Alpha and the Omega, the first and the last (Rev. 22:13). He can override any grim diagnosis, any death report—and this is what He has promised in His Word:

> "*With long life I will satisfy him*, and show him My salvation." (Ps. 91:16)

God's heart is never for you to die young, nor for you to live a long but miserable life. He wants you to live a long, satisfying life full of His goodness, wholeness, and peace. If you are not satisfied with the current length of your life, tell Him. And by the way, when He declared, "With long life I will satisfy him, and show him My salvation," the Hebrew word for *salvation* here is the word *yeshua*,[2] and that's the name of Jesus. God will satisfy you with a long, full life where you walk in all the blessings of health, wholeness, and provision you have in Christ. Whatever your circumstances might look like on the outside, keep standing on His promises.

> **GOD'S HEART IS FOR YOU TO LIVE A LONG, SATISFYING LIFE FULL OF HIS GOODNESS, WHOLENESS, AND PEACE.**

JESUS REVEALED THE FATHER'S HEART FOR YOU

How do you know it is God's will to heal you? Just look at what Jesus did during His earthly ministry. When we look at Jesus, we see our heavenly Father's heart for us, as Jesus said, "He who has seen Me has seen the Father" (John 14:9).

Throughout the Gospels, what do we see Jesus tirelessly doing?

And Jesus went about all Galilee, teaching in their synagogues, preaching the gospel of the kingdom, and healing all kinds of sickness and all kinds of disease among the people. Then His fame went throughout all Syria; and they brought to Him all sick people who were afflicted with various diseases and torments, and those who were demon-possessed, epileptics, and paralytics; and He healed them. (Matt. 4:23–24)

Then great multitudes came to Him, having with them the lame, blind, mute, maimed, and many others; and they laid them down at Jesus' feet, and He healed them. (Matt. 15:30)

When the sun was setting, all those who had any that were sick with various diseases brought them to Him; and He laid His hands on every one of them and healed them. (Luke 4:40)

Over and over again, the Bible records how our Lord Jesus "went about doing good and *healing all* who were oppressed by the devil" (Acts 10:38). He caused the lame to walk and the blind to see. He unstopped deaf ears. He cleansed people with leprosy. He even raised the dead.

> **IT IS YOUR HEAVENLY FATHER'S DESIRE FOR YOU TO BE COMPLETELY HEALED OF EVERY DISEASE.**

And do you know what our Lord Jesus said about all that He did? He said, "The words I say to you I do not say on My own initiative or authority, but the Father, abiding continually in Me, does His works [His attesting miracles and acts of power]" (John 14:10 AMP).

Jesus said it was *the Father* who worked (through Him) wonderful healing miracles everywhere He went. Can you see that it is truly your heavenly Father's desire for you to be completely healed of every disease?

The devil may have stolen man's confidence

in a good God, but when Jesus came, He not only restored the image of a good God but also revealed to us a God who is a loving Father.

YOUR FATHER WANTS YOU HEALED

As a father, it always pains me to see my children unwell. My firstborn daughter, Jessica, is all grown up now, but I remember how it broke my heart to see her bawling when she was suffering from viral fever as a baby. I remember cradling her in my arms and praying over her as I paced around her room the whole night. As long as she was sick, I could not rest.

I sponged her feverish body over and over again. I sang to her in an attempt to soothe her. I hated the fever that was causing my baby to convulse in pain. I would have done anything to alleviate her discomfort. If I could have taken her fever and put it on my own body so she would not have to go through the pain, I would gladly have done so.

What I feel when my children are unwell is only a microcosmic reflection of what our heavenly Father feels for us when we are unwell. He wants us brimming with health and life. He hates sicknesses and diseases because of what they do to us. But the difference is this: He was able to take our sicknesses, and He put them on Jesus' own body as He hung on the cross, so that we would not have to suffer them. The Bible tells us:

He Himself took our infirmities and bore our sicknesses. (Matt. 8:17)

Why did our Lord Jesus do that? Because He loves us so much. He could not rest until He had secured our salvation, our health, and our wholeness. Finally, when He had borne every sin, every disease, and every infirmity upon His own body, He cried, "It is finished!" (John 19:30) and rested.

HE FREELY GIVES YOU HEALING

Isaiah 53:5 tells us that by Jesus' stripes we are healed. Every stripe He bore as He was scourged was for our healing. And He willingly allowed stripe after stripe to rip into His body so you and I could be well. Don't ever believe the enemy's lie that God wants you sick or that He is not willing to heal you. At the cross, our Lord Jesus demonstrated once and for all that He wants you well.

The Bible even tells us that it pleased the Lord to "crush Him" (Isa. 53:10 NASB). I used to wonder how it could have pleased the Lord to crush His own Son. Then one day, the Lord showed me.

EVERY STRIPE HE BORE WAS FOR OUR HEALING.

My wife, Wendy, and I had gone to a mall and the nearest parking lot we could find was quite a distance away. We did a lot of shopping that day and before we knew it, we had our hands full of shopping bags. By this time, my Jessica, who was a cherubic two-year-old then, was tired and wanted to be carried. I picked her up with one arm, and she was so exhausted she fell asleep on my shoulder almost immediately.

As we walked toward our car, I felt my arm go to sleep, and I realized the car was much farther away than I had thought. It felt like a million pins and needles were piercing my arm, and I knew I could stop the burning pain by simply putting Jessica down and making her walk the rest of the way. But she was sleeping so soundly and deeply I could not bear to put her down. I loved her so much I was willing to "crush" my arm so my little darling could continue to sleep.

All of a sudden I began to understand how it could please God to crush Jesus, who is described in the same chapter as "the arm of the LORD" (Isa. 53:1). It pleased the Lord to crush His only begotten Son because of His great love for you and me. That was the only way God could save us from sin and disease, and He willingly chose to give up His Son.

Today you can have full assurance God wants to heal you. The Bible tells us:

He who did not spare His own Son, but delivered Him up for us all, how shall He not with Him also freely give us all things? (Rom. 8:32)

God already gave us the best of heaven when He gave us His darling Jesus. What are our temporal needs when He has already given us a gift that is eternal? Whatever your needs are, whether it is financial provision or healing for your body, they are all lesser compared to the gift of His Son. How shall He not with Him also freely give them to you? God will not withhold His healing from you. In fact, He has already paid the price for your healing. Your part is to keep believing and keep trusting until you see the full manifestation of your healing.

NEVER GOD'S WILL FOR YOU TO BE SICK

God is a good God, and He loves us so much. That is why I cannot understand why there are those who teach that God sometimes uses sickness to teach us a lesson or that we need to "pray hard" for His healing. Can you imagine any earthly father inflicting suffering on his own child? Must you be persuaded to alleviate your child's pain? There are even some people who claim that it is sometimes God's will for us to be sick. But when their own children fall sick, they do everything within their power to ensure their children recover. If it were really God's will for us to be sick, seeking recovery would be deliberately trying to get out of God's will!

HE HAS ALREADY PAID THE PRICE. YOUR PART IS TO KEEP BELIEVING UNTIL YOU SEE THE FULL MANIFESTATION OF YOUR HEALING.

If earthly, fallible parents want the best for their children, how much more our heavenly Father? He wants us strong, well, and enjoying life. Our Lord Jesus said it like this: "If you then, being evil, know how to give good gifts to your children, how much more will your Father who is in heaven give good things to those who ask Him!" (Matt. 7:11).

You will *never* find Jesus looking at a person and saying, "Come here. You are too healthy. Receive some leprosy." You will never find Jesus saying, "My Father is chastising you, that's why you are sick." You know why? Because God does *not* give sicknesses and diseases.

> STOP BELIEVING THAT SICKNESS IS PART OF GOD'S WILL. GOD WANTS YOU WELL!

Jesus taught us to pray, "Your will be done on earth as it is in heaven" (Matt. 6:10). Do you think there is death or decay in heaven? Are there hospitals or cemeteries in heaven? If sickness, disease, and death were God's will, heaven would be filled with them. But we know it is not. So let's stop believing that sickness is part of God's will. If there is a condition in your body, may this truth be burned into your heart right now: *God wants you well!*

BOY HEALED OF SCOLIOSIS

I want to share with you a precious testimony from Caleb, a father in Texas who wrote to my team:

> My youngest son was diagnosed with scoliosis when his X-ray showed a seventeen-degree curve in his spine. Upon receiving the news, fear, doubt, anger, sadness, worry, and condemnation began to set in our hearts. We were also concerned about potential disabilities and surgeries for our son in the future.
>
> As a pastor, I found myself struggling with my Christian beliefs. Nevertheless, I could feel the Lord's loving embrace and peace as I prayed for my son. My church also prayed for him, and we believed the Lord could, and would, heal him.
>
> The doctor referred him to a children's hospital and

arranged for an appointment. By faith, we decided to go for the appointment to confirm the healing had already begun. Even though doubt, condemnation, and fear crept into our hearts, we kept declaring the finished work of the cross and we kept partaking of the holy Communion.

During the appointment, the doctor examined my son and took more X-rays. Then she said, "I have good news for you!" and showed us the X-rays that displayed *no* trace of scoliosis. Our son's spine had straightened out. The Lord had healed him! There is victory and power in the cross indeed!

We now distribute a copy of Pastor Prince's book *The Power of Right Believing* to every new member in our church. We believe miracles happen as we fill ourselves with the good news of the gospel.

I really felt for Caleb when he described the feelings he went through on hearing his son was diagnosed with scoliosis. I believe every loving parent would be in turmoil if their child were diagnosed with a condition that could potentially lead to lifelong disability. Every parent wants their child to be well and to enjoy a quality life, and that's also our heavenly Father's heart toward us.

Despite his fears and uncertainties, Caleb did the best thing he could for his son. He kept declaring the finished work of the cross, and he kept partaking of the holy Communion.

And just like that, with nothing spectacular happening, no voice booming out from heaven, and no earth-shaking demonstration of power, his son was healed.

> YOUR HEAVENLY FATHER WANTS YOU WELL AND ENJOYING A QUALITY LIFE.

Caleb, as I look again at the copies of your son's X-rays showing a perfectly healed and normal spine, I am rejoicing with you. Thank you for sending me not just your written testimony but also copies of the

X-rays taken of your son when he was first diagnosed with scoliosis, as well as the one showing his spine straightened. The enemy tried to destroy your son, but the Lord healed him completely. I pray that in the days ahead, the Lord will use your son mightily as a testimony of His healing power and bring encouragement to many.

BE ROOTED IN HIS LOVE

My friend, if you have received a negative report, it is natural for you to be fearful. Notice that Caleb felt fear, doubt, anger, sadness, worry, and condemnation, and he even "struggled with his Christian beliefs." The Lord does not expect you to never be shaken. But in the midst of your tumult of emotions, keep your eyes on Jesus, and like Caleb, keep on declaring His finished work over your situation.

Maybe right now you are angry with God for allowing a disease to take root in the body of a loved one. Maybe you are feeling helpless because it feels as if you are standing on the sidelines, and there is nothing you can do to alleviate the suffering. Or maybe you yourself have been confined to a hospital bed, and you are terrified. Every time you are wheeled out for more scans, you don't know what the doctors will find, and you are crying out, "God, why is this happening to me? Where are You?"

KEEP YOUR EYES ON JESUS AND KEEP DECLARING HIS FINISHED WORK OVER YOUR SITUATION.

When you are staring at the symptoms in your body or in the body of your loved one, when it seems like you have prayed with all your heart and still the sickness remains, I know it is hard to believe God can heal. Or maybe you believe He can heal, but you doubt He wants to. Perhaps you have given up hope because you think that if He wanted to heal you or your loved one, He would have done it already.

If that is how you feel right now, may I encourage you to *feed on His love for you*. The doubts in your mind might be screaming so loudly it's hard for you to even believe in Him anymore. But I pray that you will be able to catch a fresh glimpse of the width and length and depth and height of your Savior's love for you (Eph. 3:18–19). I pray that even when your mind cannot understand it, your heart will be rooted and established in His love for you. When you are so established in His love, you will see Him do exceedingly, abundantly, above all that you ask or think (Eph. 3:20).

Do not allow the enemy to shake your faith. Do not allow the enemy to sell you any more lies. He is a defeated foe, and whatever evil he meant against you, God will turn it around for your good and for His glory. The Word of God declares that *"no weapon formed against you shall prosper"* (Isa. 54:17). Even if the enemy has formed some weapon of disease against you, believe it has no power to prosper and prevail against you.

> **WHEN YOU ARE ESTABLISHED IN HIS LOVE, YOU WILL SEE HIM DO EXCEEDINGLY, ABUNDANTLY, ABOVE ALL THAT YOU CAN ASK OR THINK.**

You have a heavenly Father who loves you so much He gave up His own Son for you. The devil wants you to be disillusioned and to turn away from God, but, my friend, *now* is the time you need to turn to Him more than ever before. Now is the time you need to trust your Savior. Now is the time for you to take your authority as a child of the Most High God, and to claim every promise in the Scriptures of health and long life that Jesus died to give you!

NO PLACE FOR FEAR

Down through the years, as I minister to precious people, I have seen how fear can creep in when someone is diagnosed with a condition or when loved ones develop serious illnesses. If you know someone who is experiencing this, you can encourage them with this verse from 2 Timothy, which declares that "God has not given us a spirit of fear, but of power and of love and of a sound mind" (2 Tim. 1:7). Because of what Jesus did on the cross, we do not have to remain apprehensive, but can trust the Lord to come to a place where there is no room in our hearts for fear, knowing that His perfect love drives out every fear from our hearts (1 John 4:18).

> **HIS PERFECT LOVE DRIVES OUT EVERY FEAR FROM OUR HEARTS.**

I understand that finding out you or your loved one has a medical condition can be frightening. Maybe you have just discovered in your body a lump that was never there before, or you can no longer ignore worrying symptoms like the pain that won't go away, the blurred vision you keep experiencing, or the waves of nausea that have been hitting you. Maybe your thoughts are completely out of control and you cannot help but imagine the worst as you await the results of yet another round of MRI scans, blood work, or other tests you don't understand.

Maybe you have already been given a diagnosis and it is worse than what you had imagined. Now it feels like you cannot breathe, and you are trying your best not to panic, but it is so hard. Questions keep hurtling through your mind and you have no answers, only more questions.

What if I have the same condition my mother died of?

How am I going to afford the treatment?

Who is going to look after my kids?

How long do I have?

If I go through with that treatment, what is going to happen to me? Will I lose all my hair? Will I ever be the same again?

Why? Why me?

You may even have friends and family members who are trying to reassure you things will be okay, but their words sound empty to you. How could they understand? How can they say things will be okay? They are not the ones struggling to remember even their own child's name. They are not the ones whose bodies have to be cut open. They are not the ones who will have radiation blasting through their bodies. They are not the ones who have to watch helplessly as their child is wheeled in for yet another surgery.

How can they tell you not to worry and to have faith when they have no idea what it feels like to be suffocating from the chilling dread of getting yet another bad report after praying and believing there would finally be some good news? How can they tell you to not be afraid when they don't know how it feels to have to go through another cycle of chemotherapy or to realize you are losing so much strength you have to struggle just to sit up?

YOUR SYMPTOMS ARE REAL. BUT THE POWER OF GOD IS EVEN MORE REAL.

Fear can overwhelm you like a tsunami. It can paralyze you. It can cause you to become angry. Angry at life. At God. At everyone.

Maybe you know exactly what I mean.

If you do, may I ask you to please read on? I believe the Lord has a word for you.

FOCUS ON GOD'S PROMISES, NOT THE DISEASE

The tumor, the dialysis machine, and the feeding tube are real. But it is so important for you to know this: the power of God is even *more* real.

Do you know what happens if you hold up a dime and bring it right up to one of your eyes while keeping the other eye closed? That small dime appears so big it can block your view of everything else. As long as you keep focusing on that dime, you are effectively blinded. That, my friend, is what the enemy is trying to do to you right now.

The enemy wants you to be intensely focused on the disease, the devastating medical report, the incessant beeping of the monitors around you, and the sterile smell of the hospital room. He wants you to be completely fixated on the fears and questions that keep screaming in your mind. As long as all you can see is your pain, your dread, your disappointment, and your suffering, he has the upper hand.

> **AS LONG AS ALL YOU CAN SEE IS YOUR PAIN AND SUFFERING, THE ENEMY HAS THE UPPER HAND.**

And do you know why the enemy is bent on keeping you absorbed in the challenge you are facing? Because he is afraid you will see he has already been defeated.

The Bible tells us that at the cross, our Lord Jesus disarmed all principalities and powers, made a public spectacle of them, and triumphed over them (Col. 2:15). The enemy has been disarmed. He has been stripped of his weapons (this includes all kinds of sickness and disease) against you. You do not need to fear him, child of the Most High!

The devil will keep trying to deceive and distract you from this truth. He will keep trying to get you to focus on the temporal, visible things around you. He does not want you to see the things that are eternal, like the angels that have been instructed to watch over you and keep you in all your ways (Ps. 91:11). Like the Word of God that will never pass away (Matt. 24:35) and declares that by His stripes *you are healed* (Isa. 53:5).

> **THE ENEMY HAS BEEN DISARMED. YOU DO NOT NEED TO FEAR HIM, CHILD OF THE MOST HIGH!**

MORE WITH YOU THAN AGAINST YOU

The Bible records what happened when Israel's enemies tried to capture the prophet Elisha while he was in the city of Dothan. A great army with horses and chariots came by night and surrounded the city. When Elisha's servant woke up, he despaired and cried out, "What shall we do?" (2 Kings 6:14–15).

May I invite you to read for yourself what happened next?

> So he [Elisha] answered, *"Do not fear, for those who are with us are more than those who are with them."* And Elisha prayed, and said, "Lord, I pray, open his eyes that he may see." Then the Lord opened the eyes of the young man, and he saw. And behold, the mountain was full of horses and chariots of fire all around Elisha. (2 Kings 6:16–17)

It may feel like a formidable army of symptoms, negative reports, and maybe even financial debt has surrounded you. But, beloved, do not fear, for those who are *with you* are *so much more* than those who are with them.

Right now, I pray that the Lord will open your eyes so you might see the legions of angels stationed around you. Take your eyes off your enemies. The ability of your enemies to hurt you is *nothing* compared to the greatness of your God and His power to save you. Take your eyes off the enemy so you may see the exceeding greatness of God's power toward you. The same mighty power that raised our Lord Jesus from the grave, the same power that seated Him at God's right hand in the heavenly places—far above all principalities, power, might, and dominion, and every name that is named, not only in this age but also in the age to come (Eph. 1:19–21)—is working *for* you and for your loved one!

> THE ABILITY OF YOUR ENEMIES TO HURT YOU IS *NOTHING* COMPARED TO GOD'S POWER TO SAVE YOU.

Is human papillomavirus a name? Is bacterial meningitis a name? Is Parkinson's disease a name? Then it has to yield to Jesus, who is seated at the Father's right hand, far above the diseases. And as He is, so are you in this world (1 John 4:17).

HOW TO DRIVE OUT EVERY FEAR

As you wait for the doctor's verdict on the nature of those cells he saw in your scan, or as you look at the dark mass in your X-ray, you can't help but be filled with trepidation. You try telling yourself not to be fearful, but you can't seem to stop fearing. Do you know why? Because you cannot reason your way out of fear. Fear is not logical.

The only way to get fear out of your life is to cast it out, and the Bible tells us how:

> There is no fear in love; but *perfect love casts out fear*, because fear involves torment. (1 John 4:18)

You cast out fear by exposing yourself to the perfect love of God. Keep allowing His love to inundate you and drive out every fear. The

Bible talks about keeping ourselves in the love of
God (Jude 1:21). Instead of focusing on the pain in
your body or the sickness causing your loved one
to suffer, keep yourself in His love. Set your mind
on the infallible, inexhaustible, and perfect love of
your heavenly Father.

YOU CAST OUT FEAR BY EXPOSING YOURSELF TO THE PERFECT LOVE OF GOD.

You have a God who loves you so much He
gave His Son to die on the cross for you. That,
my friend, is why you can always have rock-solid
assurance you are loved by Him. The Bible defines
His love for us like this:

> God showed how much he loved us by sending his one and only Son
> into the world so that we might have eternal life through him. This
> is real love—not that we loved God, but that he loved us and sent his
> Son as a sacrifice to take away our sins. (1 John 4:9–10 NLT)

The cross is everlasting proof of God's love for you. The cross is
the measure of how much He loves you. You must never judge His love
based on your circumstances. The devil can attack your circumstances,
but he can never attack the cross. Take your eyes off your circumstances
and put them on the cross. That's where God's love for you was demonstrated once and for all!

HOW TO KEEP YOURSELF IN HIS PERFECT LOVE

I know it can be very hard to *feel* God's love for you when you are faced
with multiple symptoms in your body, mounting debts from your medical
bills, and worries about your future. We live in a world where we are
governed by our five senses, and the truth is, there are times when it
is hard to believe in the love of Someone we can't see, touch, or hear.
But we cannot depend on feelings and outward circumstances (that can

change) to be assured of God's love for us. It is so important we fix our eyes, instead, on our Lord Jesus, whose love for us is perfect, never changes, and never fails.

May I share with you some of the things you can do that I believe will help to keep you in His love?

NEVER JUDGE GOD'S LOVE FOR YOU BASED ON YOUR CIRCUMSTANCES.

Instead of allowing the enemy to feed you with lies that cause you to be fearful, may I encourage you to keep listening to messages that will keep you in the consciousness of God's love for you? Embrace His love to drive out every fear. Every time the enemy tries to attack you with fears, plug into a sermon that magnifies the Lord's goodness and His love for you. Instead of giving in to the devices of the enemy, keep listening to sermons about Jesus' finished work.

Whenever fear tries to creep up on you, go somewhere quiet and meditate on how much the Lord loves you as you partake of the holy Communion. Talk to your Savior, and as you lift up the bread, tell Him, "Lord Jesus, thank You that You love me so much You allowed Your body to be broken so mine can be whole. Right now, I receive Your wholeness, Your strength, and Your divine health." As you lift up the cup, say, "Thank You for Your precious blood, which has cleansed me of every sin. Right now, I can come boldly to Your throne of grace, knowing I am completely righteous, knowing my prayers avail much!"

When you partake of the Communion, you are "proclaiming the Lord's death" (1 Cor. 11:26) and reminding the devil and his cohorts of their humiliating defeat at the cross (Col. 2:15). You are proclaiming to the enemy that he has *no* right to put symptoms or sicknesses on your body because your Lord Jesus has already borne every disease and pain on His own body.

Instead of reading articles on the internet that tell you how serious your condition can become, or reading your medical report over and over again, read praise reports about the Lord's love and faithfulness.[1] Read scriptures about His love and healing promises. Garrison yourself with the Word of God and keep yourself in His love.

The Bible tells us, "And we have *known and believed* the love that God has for us. God is love, and *he who abides in love abides in God, and God in him*" (1 John 4:16). It's not enough to know verses *about* His love. Keep meditating on them until you *believe* He loves you. When we keep ourselves in the consciousness of God's love for us, we are abiding in God. In other words, we are making Him our dwelling place. That is so powerful because when the Lord is your dwelling place, you are in a place of safety and protection.

> **GARRISON YOURSELF WITH THE WORD OF GOD AND KEEP YOURSELF IN HIS LOVE.**

Read Psalm 91 and declare over yourself that no evil shall befall you nor shall any plague come near your dwelling. As you abide in Him, the almighty God becomes your refuge and fortress. It doesn't matter how many people have died from the disease you have been diagnosed with. A thousand may fall at your side and ten thousand at your right hand, but it shall not come near you (Ps. 91:7). And even if you are already in trouble, the Lord is with you and He will deliver you.

KEEP YOUR EYES ON THE ONE WHOSE LOVE ENDURES FOREVER

Take time to worship the Lord, *especially when* it feels like overwhelming odds are against you. Do what King Jehoshaphat did when his enemies joined forces and amassed a formidable army to destroy Israel. In the natural, Jehoshaphat knew Israel had no chance of winning the battle. But he chose to do something you and I need to learn to do whenever we are besieged by our enemies. He cried out to the Lord, saying, *"We do not know what to do, but our eyes are on you"* (2 Chron. 20:12 NIV).

Jehoshaphat then placed not commandos but worshipers at the head of his army, and this is what they sang: "Give thanks to the LORD, for *his love endures forever*" (2 Chron. 20:21 NIV).

Instead of despairing because of their enemies, they chose to fix their eyes on the Lord, giving thanks to Him and singing of His love. This happened long before the cross of Jesus. How much more can you and I sing of His love, which never fails, which endures forever!

And do you know what happened? The Lord defeated Israel's enemies by turning them against each other, and Jehoshaphat's troops did not even have to lift a finger to fight. Instead, when they turned up at the place that was supposed to be their battleground, their enemies were already dead, and all they ended up doing was collecting their plunder of equipment, clothing, and valuable items. In fact, the Bible records there was so much plunder they spent three days collecting the spoils. This is such a powerful account, and I hope you will read the details for yourself in 2 Chronicles 20:1–30.

In Jesus' name, may this happen to you too. When you are overwhelmed by challenges, and you don't know what to do or even how to feel, just cry out to the Lord and tell Him, "Lord, I don't know what to do, but my eyes are on You." That's the

THE LORD HIMSELF WILL FIGHT YOUR BATTLE.

most powerful posture you can take, with your eyes fixed not on your enemies but on your Savior. As you focus on His love that endures forever, the Lord Himself will fight your battle for you (2 Chron. 20:15). May you be so conscious of His perfect love that every fear is driven from your life, and may you walk away so much stronger than before your enemies tried to come against you!

GOD'S LOVE LEAVES NO PLACE FOR FEAR

Your heavenly Father cares about every minute detail of your life. There is nothing too big or too small for Him. Whether it's a simple pimple or a disturbing growth in your body, if it matters to you, it matters to your Daddy God. Our Lord Jesus tells us, *"The very hairs of your head are all numbered.* Do not fear therefore" (Luke 12:7). I find that so amazing—your Abba loves you so much He takes time to count the very hairs on your head!

I love my daughter, Jessica, and my son, Justin, very much, but I have never counted nor kept a record of how many strands of hair they have on their heads. Apparently, most people have an average of about one hundred thousand hair follicles and lose between fifty and one hundred hairs each day.[2] So even if I tried counting how many hairs my kids have, the numbers would constantly change. Yet the Lord knows precisely how many hairs are on each of our heads at any moment.

> EVERY LITTLE DETAIL ABOUT YOUR BODY MATTERS TO HIM.

How much more do you think it matters to Him when your body is under attack by a sickness that robs you of your health? Beloved, He loves you so much, and every one of your cells, every tissue, and every organ in your body matters to Him. Do not fear, for the Lord Himself—the One who feeds the birds of the air and clothes the flowers of the field—takes care of you (Matt. 6:25–33). Every time you are fearful, turn to His perfect love that drives out every fear.

GOD DESIRES FOR YOU TO PROSPER AND BE IN HEALTH

As I write this book, the Lord has been speaking to me about healing in a very strong way. He has led me to read a verse I believe articulates clearly His will for us. It was written by the disciple whom Jesus loved, the disciple who was an eyewitness as Jesus went about healing all who came to Him, the disciple who leaned on Jesus' bosom and knew the heartbeat of His love:

Beloved, I pray that you may prosper in all things *and be in health,* just as your soul prospers. (3 John 1:2)

What I want you to see is this: John was writing to the well-beloved Gaius, a believer. John knew that Gaius's soul was already prospering. If you have invited Jesus into your heart to be your Lord and Savior, then you have received the gift of eternal life and can have full assurance that heaven is your home (Rom. 10:9–11). Whatever challenges you might be faced with on the outside, your soul, which is eternal, has begun prospering. But it wasn't enough for John to know Gaius's soul was prospering. John prayed that Gaius would also "prosper in all things and be in health." In other words, you can pray for your outward, physical body to be healthy even as your soul is healthy in Christ.

You can be sure God's will is for you to be healthy because His Word declares it. Since His will is for you to be "in health," don't go with human tradition or man's opinion that says it is sometimes His will for you to be sick. Don't let man's conjectures and theories cause you to believe the lie that maybe God wants you to endure the sickness in your body so you can learn to trust Him more or grow in patience. Because of what Jesus did at Calvary, we can be sure sickness is *never* from God. Healing is!

Come back to the simplicity of declaring like a child, "Jesus loves me, this I know, for the Bible tells me so." In the same way, how do I know Jesus wants us walking in His health and wholeness? For the Bible tells me so.

WHY AM I NOT AUTOMATICALLY HEALED?

You might be wondering, *If God loves me, and it's His will to heal me, why am I not automatically healed? Why do I even have to pray or partake of the Communion?*

My friend, we know it is God's will for *everyone* to receive salvation, to receive the gift of eternal life that was freely given to the world (John 3:16). But nobody gets saved "automatically," because we all have the choice to accept or reject God's offer. God is a gentleman, and He will not force His salvation on anyone. He will not force His gifts on us. He will not force His blessings on us. He will not force His health or goodness on us.

When we pray and partake of the holy Communion, we are actively releasing our faith to be aligned with God's will, God's Word, and God's power. We are not begging Him to heal us or trying to persuade Him to heal our loved ones—we already know it is His will to heal. Prayer is about building an intimate relationship with Him. When we pray and partake of the holy Communion, we are receiving His love for us, and receiving His healing power into our physical bodies. Talk to God today (that's what prayer is) about your health challenges, and let Him impart boldness to you and confidence in your heart that He wants you healthy.

> **HOW DO I KNOW JESUS WANTS US WALKING IN HEALTH? FOR THE BIBLE TELLS ME SO.**

HEALED OF ALZHEIMER'S AFTER PARTAKING OF COMMUNION REGULARLY

Let me share with you a praise report from Kathy, whose husband, Marcus, had been told to "get his affairs in order" after being diagnosed with Alzheimer's disease. According to the Alzheimer's Association, Alzheimer's, which is the sixth leading cause of death in the United States, is a progressive disease that worsens over time and has no cure.[3] I can only imagine the helplessness and fear Marcus and Kathy felt when they first received the diagnosis. But read on and see what the Lord did for them:

> Some years ago, during a routine checkup following a brain bleed, Marcus's doctor told us Marcus had indeed progressed

much further than she expected. However, based on his latest brain scan as well as scans from his hospital stay fourteen months earlier, she explained to us that Marcus had Alzheimer's disease. She went on to tell us that Marcus should "get his affairs in order" and begin to plan to retire permanently from his job.

> **WHEN WE PARTAKE OF THE COMMUNION, WE ARE RELEASING OUR FAITH TO BE ALIGNED WITH GOD'S WILL, WORD, AND POWER.**

Needless to say, this was a huge shock to us—one that neither of us was ready or willing to accept. But we truly gave the situation to God. There is much to say about the journey our Lord took us on, one that included your teaching as confirmation of what we believed we were hearing from Him.

Our Daddy God gave us faith, hope, and such peace during those dark times as we began to really trust Him with every aspect of our lives. It was through Scripture and your messages about the holy Communion that prompted us to begin taking the Communion at home on a regular basis. We believe that was when our future began to brighten.

Did you notice what Marcus and Kathy did? Marcus's diagnosis was a huge shock for them. But they didn't simply accept the diagnosis. They filled themselves with scriptures, they kept listening to the preached Word, and they started partaking of the holy Communion at home on a regular basis.

As they did all that, Kathy wrote that their "future began to brighten." They might have continued to see symptoms during that time, but they persisted. And when they look back today, they know their breakthrough began when they started partaking of the Communion regularly. It wasn't immediate and complete, but it *began* then.

Kathy wrote on to say that four and a half years later, Marcus underwent another MRI, and this was how his neurosurgeon responded when she saw the scan:

As she studied the scan, she looked quite perplexed before she said, "I'm looking at a very healthy brain. There is no Alzheimer's disease here. I'm removing that diagnosis completely from your medical records."

The things that are impossible with man are possible with our God (Luke 18:27)! Instead of degenerating, Marcus's brain became "very healthy," and he was completely discharged of Alzheimer's disease. Hallelujah!

No matter what diagnosis you might have received from your doctor, keep filling your heart with scriptures. Keep listening to messages about the Lord's finished work and partaking of the Communion. Keep remembering our Lord Jesus and His love for you. Each time fear threatens to consume you, run into His arms of love afresh and allow His love to cast out every fear. And even if you don't see your breakthrough happening yet, keep fighting the good fight of faith, knowing in your heart God loves you and wants you well. What He did for Marcus, He can do for you too!

> **THE THINGS THAT ARE IMPOSSIBLE WITH MAN ARE POSSIBLE WITH OUR GOD.**

6.

HE PAID THE BILL

If you or your loved one has been diagnosed with a medical condition, chances are, you are also being confronted with mounting medical bills. And health care is expensive. Globally, health care cost is projected to continue skyrocketing. In 2016 researchers found that America spent almost twice as much on health care compared to other high-income countries like Australia.[1] In 2017 total health care expenditure in America came up to $3.5 trillion or 17.9 percent of the US GDP.[2]

Maybe your take-home pay is just enough to cover your monthly living expenses and what you have been diagnosed with has put a strain on your finances. You have maxed out your credit cards to pay for hospitalization, medication, and all the scans you had to undergo, and you are now mired in debt. Perhaps you have no health insurance because you are between jobs and cannot afford it. And now, while the persistent high fever you have been suffering from worries you, you have not seen a doctor as the potential cost of seeing one worries you even more.

Beloved, do not be dismayed by all the accumulating bills. The Lord is not just *Jehovah Rapha*, the Lord your healer, He is also *Jehovah Jireh*, the Lord your provider. The Bible promises that He *"will* liberally supply (fill until full) your every need according to His riches in glory in Christ

Jesus" (Phil. 4:19 AMP). I pray that you will be so much more conscious of the abundance of His inexhaustible supply than of the demands on your finances. Don't ever feel like you have to handle the pressures all by yourself and take care of all the medical bills while ensuring your family has food to eat and clothes on their backs. Do not worry, for your heavenly Father knows you need all these things (Matt. 6:32). Let go of your worries and keep your eyes on Him. He will take care of you.

IT DOESN'T MATTER HOW LONG IT HAS BEEN

Did you know the Bible records the story of a woman who found herself in a serious financial crisis because of her long-term health condition (Mark 5:25–34)? She suffered from a hemorrhage or "flow of blood" and had been constantly bleeding for an extended period. We don't know what caused her condition. Her abnormal bleeding could have been caused by fibroids, hypothyroidism, or even cancer of the reproductive tract.

> THE LORD IS NOT JUST YOUR HEALER; HE IS ALSO YOUR PROVIDER. HE WILL TAKE CARE OF YOU.

Whatever the cause, we know it was a terrible condition that put her through much agony for twelve long years. We also know she had gone to many different doctors in her bid to be cured and had endured much suffering at their hands. Over the years, she spent everything she had to pay for her treatments, but she did not get better. In fact, her condition grew worse.

As you read this, maybe you can identify with this woman's predicament. Maybe you have been battling a medical condition for years, and your bank account has been completely depleted because of undergoing all the treatments the experts said would help you get better. You have been put through so many tests, been subject to so many probes, and tried so many "revolutionary cures," you have lost count. But each time the treatment failed, and all you have been left with is a ballooning debt and a condition that has deteriorated despite your best efforts.

Perhaps it has come to the point where you are tired of trying and tired of hoping. The disease has ravaged your body and you have neither the will nor the finances to continue fighting.

If that describes you, please know it is not by coincidence you are reading these words. I believe the Lord wanted you to read this because He loves you. Do not give up. Even if you have gone to specialist after specialist and tried various treatments to no avail, there is still hope!

And if you think you already know all about this woman's story, please keep reading. I have studied and preached it umpteen times and thought I knew it inside out. But the Lord began to highlight a certain phrase to me over and over again until I saw something I had never seen before.

> EVEN IF YOU HAVE GONE TO SPECIALIST AFTER SPECIALIST AND TRIED VARIOUS TREATMENTS TO NO AVAIL, THERE IS STILL HOPE.

I really believe what I am about to share with you will help you receive your breakthrough both in your body and in your finances. Here is the apostle Mark's account:

When she heard about Jesus, she came behind Him in the crowd and touched His garment. For she said, "If only I may touch His clothes, I shall be made well." Immediately the fountain of her blood was dried up, and she felt in her body that she was healed of the affliction. And Jesus, immediately knowing in Himself that power had gone out of Him, turned around in the crowd and said, "Who touched My clothes?" But His disciples said to Him, "You see the multitude thronging You, and You say, 'Who touched Me?'" And He looked around to see her who had done this thing. But the woman, fearing and trembling, knowing what had happened to her, came and fell down before Him and told Him the whole truth. And He said to her,

"Daughter, your faith has made you well. Go in peace, and be healed of your affliction." (Mark 5:27–34)

If you have been believing God for healing, you might be thinking, *If only I could see Jesus with my own eyes or hear Him with my own ears, then I could be healed.* The apostle Luke records that "great multitudes came together to hear, and to be healed by Him of their infirmities" (Luke 5:15). These multitudes heard Jesus themselves and they were healed. They heard, and they were healed.

But the apostle Mark's account about the woman with the issue of blood doesn't say, "When she heard Jesus."

It says, "When she heard *about* Jesus."

Hallelujah! Do you know what that means?

It means we can have the same faith this woman had just by hearing *about* Jesus.

We may not see or hear Jesus in person the way the people at the Mount of Beatitudes or in the synagogue in Capernaum did. But just by hearing *about* Jesus, we can receive the same faith and healing breakthrough the woman did—even if the conditions have been in our bodies for years, and even if doctors and expensive treatments have failed!

WHAT YOU HEAR ABOUT JESUS MATTERS

Now what do you think the woman heard about Jesus that was so powerful?

For twelve years she had been bleeding. According to Levitical law, she was "unclean." Whoever touched her or even touched anything she had sat on was also considered unclean (Lev. 15:19–25). This means for twelve years she had been shunned and ostracized. For twelve years she was not allowed to touch anyone so she would not defile them. Can you imagine living a life where every single day, you are painfully reminded of how unclean, how impure, and how disqualified you are?

But then she heard something about Jesus.

She heard something that caused hope to spring up in her jaded heart and gave her the faith to believe she would be made well simply by touching His clothes.

She heard something that gave her the boldness and resolve to press her weakened body through an entire crowd, even though Levitical law forbade her from touching anyone.

Most of all, she heard something that caused her to believe that in spite of the fact she was unclean, she could receive healing. That is what I want you to hear about our Lord Jesus today.

In spite of the fact you are unclean, in spite of the fact you have failed, in spite of the fact there is sin in your life, *you can receive healing*!

Don't allow man's traditions to keep you away from your loving Savior. Come to Him just as you are. You do not need to do anything to qualify yourself. You do not need to wash yourself clean before you can approach Him. You do not have to long for His touch from a distance, wishing you were good enough or pure enough. Come to Him with all your sins and all your burdens—He will make you clean. The same Jesus who gave His body for your healing also gave His blood for your forgiveness. Just come to Him!

YOU ARE QUALIFIED FOR EVERY BLESSING

> COME TO HIM JUST AS YOU ARE. HE WILL MAKE YOU CLEAN.

Years ago, when I first started preaching, I taught on why Christians are not healed. One of my spiritual heroes back then had said, "There's nothing wrong with God and nothing wrong with His Word. When you don't receive from God, there's something wrong with you." So that's what I taught my church too. I wanted the people in my congregation healed and whole, and that's why I taught them a list of reasons they were not receiving their healings, but that list just kept growing.

One day, when I was teaching this subject really strongly, I heard the voice of the Holy Spirit on the inside of me saying, "Stop disqualifying My people!"

I felt sad the Lord would say that to me, and I told Him, "But Lord, I love Your people. I want them well."

And the Lord said, "Then stop disqualifying My people."

I countered, "But Lord, I am not disqualifying them. I am trying to qualify them for Your healing."

As I said that to the Lord, my eyes were opened, and I repented.

I cannot qualify anyone for healing, and neither do I need to try. God has *already* qualified us through the blood of His Son.

Let me show you what the Word of God says:

> *Giving thanks to the Father who has qualified us* to be partakers of the inheritance of the saints in the light. He has delivered us from the power of darkness and conveyed us into the kingdom of the Son of His love, *in whom we have redemption through His blood, the forgiveness of sins.* (Col. 1:12–14)

Today you and I can give thanks to the Father who *has* qualified us. We are *already* qualified to partake of every blessing.

And not only that, He has already *delivered* us from the power of darkness and conveyed us into the kingdom of the Son of His love. Don't you love how the Bible says it? We are now in the kingdom of the Son of His love, and that means the devil no longer has any hold over us. He has *no* power over us. He has no authority to rob us of our health.

Whatever sin you might have committed, whatever mistakes you might have made, stop

GOD HAS ALREADY QUALIFIED US THROUGH THE BLOOD OF HIS SON TO PARTAKE OF EVERY BLESSING.

disqualifying yourself. Nothing you can do is so powerful it can wash away the finished work of Christ.

Maybe you don't think you deserve to be healed. Maybe you think you deserve this sickness in your body. After all, you chose to fill your body with all that unhealthy junk food for years. After all, you have not been exercising. After all, that sickness is a result of your bad decisions.

Am I saying you shouldn't eat healthily or take care of your body? Absolutely not. What I am saying is that even if you have made mistakes, you don't have to disqualify yourself. That's what grace is about—*grace is for the undeserving!*

> **GRACE IS FOR THE UNDESERVING.**

There is nothing wrong with God, nothing wrong with His Word, and definitely nothing wrong with you because Jesus has effectively and perfectly removed all your sins through His blood. Now receive your healing.

You can boldly declare, "Yes" and "Amen" to *all* the promises of God in Christ (2 Cor. 1:20). He has already qualified you to freely receive His healing, His provision for your financial needs, His favor, His joy, and His peace.

DELIVERED FROM ADDICTIONS AND HEPATITIS C

Shirley from Texas wrote to share her testimony with my team, and I wanted to share some of it here because in the natural, there were many things in her life that would have disqualified her from receiving God's healing, according to what many believe.

For ten years, Shirley was addicted to drugs and alcohol. As a result of this lifestyle, she contracted hepatitis C, a serious and unfortunately silent liver disease, which is chronic and sometimes fatal. A year later, upon another test, she was still reactive with the hepatitis C virus.

Shirley shared how even though the Lord had delivered her from her addictions (and she has been sober since then), she felt she had fallen short as a Christian even when she was trying her best. She kept feeling that she could have prayed more, read the Bible more, gone to church more.

Then she heard me share the gospel and about the holy Communion. In her own words, that brought the "radical grace of God" into her situation. She wrote to tell us what had happened:

> I began listening to Joseph Prince and attending Grace Revolution Church in Dallas. I also began partaking of the holy Communion at home and to stand on Jesus' finished work whenever I received the Communion.
>
> Sometime later, I went to see an infectious diseases specialist to do blood work in order to find out what genotype of hepatitis C I had to get the right treatment. A few weeks later, I received a call from the doctor to say she had good news for me: I was a rare individual because I had developed antibodies against the virus and was now immune to it. She told me that my body had fought the virus off and I didn't need any treatments. Praise Jesus! All glory to Him! As Jesus is, so am I in this world. As He doesn't have hepatitis C in His blood, neither do I!
>
> What is so neat about this is I felt I had not been spending as much time with God as I would have liked to. I felt like I had fallen short as a Christian. I hadn't even been to church that much. This is a strong message for me—that there is nothing I can do to earn my healing or right standing with the Father. The fact I have felt less spiritual over the past year but was still healed is a powerful testament to the radical grace of our Lord Jesus Christ.
>
> On top of that, I have not gotten sick with a cold or anything else all year. Normally, I get sick at least three to four times during the winter months. Every time I felt like I was

starting to get sick, I would claim Jesus' finished work over my body. I would wake up the next morning healed and refreshed! Praise God!

Thank you so much, Pastor Prince, for the amazing message of God's grace that has changed my life. Thank you for opening my eyes to the power of Jesus' finished work and His *agape* love for us.

Praise the Lord! I rejoice to know Shirley is free from hepatitis C and freely enjoying the Lord's grace and love.

There were many areas of failure in Shirley's life, but what I love is how the grace of God delivered her from ten years of heavy addiction, and every desire to do drugs and drink was not able to make a comeback as she kept listening to preaching about Jesus, receiving the gift of righteousness, and partaking of the holy Communion for her healing. Truly, it is the goodness of God that leads us to repentance.

WHAT YOU HEAR ABOUT GOD COULD MEAN THE DIFFERENCE BETWEEN LIFE AND DEATH.

If Shirley had heard that she had to have her life all together before God could heal her, do you think she would have received her healing from hepatitis C or experienced greater health and protection in her body than she has ever had before?

What you hear about God could mean the difference between life and death. Are you hearing the voice of disqualification or the voice of grace that qualifies you based on the cross of Jesus?

JESUS IS ABLE AND WILLING TO HEAL YOU

You've seen how our Lord Jesus healed the woman with the issue of blood. I want to show you how Jesus healed another person who was also disqualified and considered unclean under the law. Matthew 8 takes place at the Mount of Beatitudes right after Jesus preached the Sermon on the Mount, and it opens like this:

> When He had come down from the mountain, great multitudes fol-
> lowed Him. And behold, a leper came and worshiped Him, saying,
> "Lord, if You are willing, You can make me clean." Then Jesus put
> out His hand and touched him, saying, "I am willing; be cleansed."
> Immediately his leprosy was cleansed. (Matt. 8:1–3)

Every time I get to travel to Israel with my pastors, one of my favorite places to visit is the Mount of Beatitudes. A number of years ago, we climbed up to where Jesus could have sat while He preached to the multitudes below. Then, as my pastors were talking, I left them there and walked along a path, just to spend some time with the Lord. That was when I realized the path led all the way to Capernaum.

For the longest time, I had imagined Jesus going down the mountain toward the multitude. But that day, I realized the gospel of Matthew records that when Jesus came down from the mountain, "great multi- tudes followed Him." If He had headed down toward the multitudes, it wouldn't have made sense to say they "followed" Him. Very likely, He had to be walking down another side of the mountain toward Capernaum for the multitudes to follow Him. Just one verse after Jesus healed the man with leprosy, the Bible tells us He entered Capernaum (Matt. 8:5), so I believe that's where Jesus was headed after He finished His sermon.

Anyway, I continued to walk along that path until I came to a huge pile of rocks on the side and noticed other slabs of stone strewn nearby. All of a sudden, I felt the Lord arrest me, and He began to give me an inner vision.

I saw how the man with leprosy could have hidden under those rocks so he could hear Jesus preach without being seen by the multi- tudes. Had he been seen, being unclean because of his leprosy, people repulsed by his condition might have hurled stones at him to drive him away.

I saw the anguish of the man, who was suffering not only because his body was covered with leprous sores and raw, exposed flesh but also because he was forced to isolate himself and be cut off from his loved ones so he would not contaminate or defile them (Lev. 13:45–46).

I saw the desperation of the man who threw himself before Jesus, worshiping Him as he said, "Lord, if You are willing, You can make me clean."

And I saw the beauty and the majesty of our Lord Jesus as He bent down to *touch* the man with leprosy, raise him up, and pronounce, "I am willing; be cleansed."

In that moment, the Lord didn't just restore the man's health, He also restored his humanity.

I don't know if you realize how amazing it is that Jesus touched a man with leprosy. Under the law, when the clean touches the unclean, the clean becomes unclean. Our Lord Jesus was showing that under grace, when the clean (Jesus) touches the unclean, the unclean becomes clean! Jesus did not contract defilement by touching the leper—He banished it.

UNDER GRACE, WHEN THE CLEAN TOUCHES THE UNCLEAN, THE UNCLEAN BECOMES CLEAN!

Based on what I saw in the Spirit, I worked with my team to prepare a video of the healing of the man with leprosy so you can experience it, too, and I have included the URL here: JosephPrince.com/eat. Even the music you will hear when you watch the video was from heaven. I sang a spontaneous song in the Spirit during one of our midweek services, and we decided later to use the melody for the video. As you watch it, may you sense the depths of our Lord's compassion and feel His tender love for you. May you see that His holiness is a holiness that can be approached, and may you see Him coming to you, seeking you out, and lifting you out from your pain.

STOP DISQUALIFYING YOURSELF

There are many people who believe God has the power to heal. But like the man with leprosy, they doubt that God is willing to use His power to heal them. If you have ever entertained such doubts about His willingness to heal you, may it forever be settled in your heart as you hear Jesus say to you, "I am willing, be cleansed! Be healed!" Your sins and shortcomings do not repulse Jesus. On the contrary, the very things you believe disqualify you *qualify* you for His saving grace. As you worship Him and look away from your disqualifications, let Him touch you and make you clean.

SEE JESUS COMING TO YOU, SEEKING YOU OUT, AND LIFTING YOU OUT FROM YOUR PAIN.

Healing is a grace gift. You cannot earn healing by your good works, and neither can your shortcomings cause you to be disqualified from receiving it. Just think about every person whom Jesus healed. Of the great multitudes that were healed, don't you think there were people who had sin and failures in their lives? Did any of those whom Jesus healed have to do anything to earn or qualify for their healing first?

Beloved, stop disqualifying yourself. No matter how you think you have failed, no matter how dirty and unclean you think you are, God loves you. Just as He cleansed the man with leprosy and healed the woman with the issue of blood, He can heal you, and He is most willing. Under the law, you would be disqualified. But Jesus came to fulfill every jot and every tittle of the law (Matt. 5:17–18) so that today we can freely receive the good we do not deserve. Our Lord Jesus bore our sins as well as our sicknesses on the cross. When God looks at you, He does not see your sins and failures. If you have accepted Jesus into your heart, you are a new creation in Christ (2 Cor. 5:17). Come boldly and receive help for every need (Heb. 4:16)!

I pray that today you have heard about a Jesus who freely releases blessings, provision, and healing with a lavish hand that does not hold back. I pray that you have seen a Jesus who demonstrated His willingness to take your sicknesses and uncleanness and give you His divine health and righteousness in exchange.

WHAT'S BETTER THAN HAVING JESUS IN PERSON

But maybe you still have doubts about your healing.

You saw how Jesus healed the woman of a chronic, long-term affliction and cleansed the man of an incurable disease. Perhaps you are thinking, *Yes, but they met Jesus in person. If I could just meet Jesus in person, I could be healed.*

JESUS CAME TO FULFILL EVERY JOT AND TITTLE OF THE LAW SO THAT WE CAN FREELY RECEIVE THE GOOD WE DO NOT DESERVE.

My friend, I have such good news for you.

Our Lord Jesus Himself told His disciples, "It is to your advantage that I go away; for if I do not go away, the Helper will not come to you; but if I depart, I will send Him to you" (John 16:7). When Jesus was on earth, He was limited. He could only be at one place at a time. But now that He has sent us the Holy Spirit, it is to our advantage! He is completely unlimited, and He can say this to you and me:

"I am with you always, even to the end of the age." (Matt. 28:20)

Hallelujah! Jesus is, right now—in the present tense—*with* you and me. He is not far away. Wherever we may be and whatever circumstances we might face, He is with us. Our part is to come *boldly* to Him to receive His mercy, His grace, and His help (Heb. 4:16). Don't disqualify yourself anymore or allow anyone to tell you that you do not deserve His gift of healing. Come boldly to Him today.

And that's not all. Did you notice that the woman with the issue of blood was healed just by touching Jesus' clothes? Today you have something *far* better than His clothes. You get to partake of *Jesus' body* in a tangible and practical way.

> **WHATEVER CIRCUMSTANCES WE MIGHT FACE, HE IS WITH US.**

What do I mean by this? On the night our Lord Jesus was betrayed, He instituted the holy Communion. He took bread and the Bible tells us this:

> When He had given thanks, He broke it and said, "Take, eat; *this is My body which is broken for you*; do this in remembrance of Me." In the same manner He also took the cup after supper, saying, "This cup is the new covenant in My blood. This do, as often as you drink it, in remembrance of Me." (1 Cor. 11:24–25)

Every time we partake of the holy Communion, we are partaking of Jesus' own body and we are receiving His blood. If even His garments contained such healing virtue, can you imagine what power is packed into the holy Communion? There is so much I want to share with you about the healing power of the holy Communion, and I cannot wait to dive further in!

7.

REVELATION BRINGS RESULTS

If you have been reading this book from the start, I pray that you have begun to see that *whatever* medical condition you or your loved one might have, there is hope.

There is hope because you are *not* on your own, and you are *not your own*—you belong to a God who loves you with a love so intense that you could never comprehend the length and breadth and depth and height of His exceeding love toward you. It is a love that surpasses knowledge, a love that is too great to ever understand (Eph. 3:18–19).

There is hope because you belong to a God who could not leave you to suffer disease and sickness and sent His own beloved Son to bear *all* your pains and your sicknesses upon His own body.

There is hope because you belong to a God who has given you a practical way by which you can have access to His healing power *any time*. You can come to Him freely. There are no religious hoops to jump through, no qualifications you have to meet. He has *already* qualified you, and the only thing you need to do is to respond to His invitation when He took the bread and said, "*Take, eat*; this is My body," when He took the cup and said, "*Drink from it*, all of you" (Matt. 26:26–27).

I pray that you have caught a revelation of *what* to eat to live a life that is brimming with vitality and have a body that is filled with divine health and strength. In this and the next chapter, I want to share with you about *how* to eat of the Lord's Supper for life and health. It might seem strange to you that I would want to write about *how* to partake of the holy Communion. Isn't it just about eating (chewing and swallowing) and drinking, which aren't exactly skills that need to be taught? My friend, partaking of

> **THERE ARE NO RELIGIOUS HOOPS TO JUMP THROUGH TO ACCESS HIS HEALING POWER.**

the Communion does involve eating and drinking. But it is completely different from any other diet you may have tried.

THE HOLY COMMUNION IS NOT ABOUT RULES AND RITUALS

Every diet and eating plan has rules you need to adhere to in order to see results and breakthroughs. Whether it is minimizing carbohydrates, loading up on proteins, portion control, or abstaining from certain foods at various timings, every diet has its own set of dos and don'ts. If you want to make any progress, you have to be disciplined enough and follow through on all the tenets of the diet. But if you take one too many "cheat days," there will be minimal or no results. The point is, the results of any diet are entirely dependent on *you*. Whether your diet works or not is dependent on fallen creation—on *your* discipline, *your* willpower, and *your* ability to maintain and keep the rules.

When it comes to the holy Communion, it has nothing to do with what you need to do, and everything to do with having a revelation of what was done *for you*. Whenever you read the Bible, remember it's not just a historical text or a record of the life of our Lord Jesus. The Bible documents His love *for you*! I pray that the Holy Spirit has given you eyes to see that all Jesus endured was *for you*. *You* and your wholeness were the joy that was set before Him. Every sacrifice He made was *for you*. The divine One suffered *for you* to have divine life, health, and wholeness!

PARTAKING IN REMEMBRANCE

I want to show you what the apostle Paul wrote about the holy Communion:

> **THE HOLY COMMUNION HAS NOTHING TO DO WITH WHAT YOU NEED TO DO, AND EVERYTHING TO DO WITH HAVING A REVELATION OF WHAT WAS DONE FOR YOU.**

For I received from the Lord that which I also delivered to you: that the Lord Jesus on the same night in which He was betrayed took bread; and when He had given thanks, He broke it and said, "Take, eat; *this is My body which is broken for you; do this in remembrance of Me.*" In the same manner He also took the cup after supper, saying, "This cup is the new covenant in My blood. This do, as often as you drink it, *in remembrance of Me*. For as often as you eat this bread and drink this cup, you proclaim the Lord's death till He comes." (1 Cor. 11:23–26)

The results for diets and exercise come from rules, routine, and regimentation. The results from the holy Communion come from relationship, revelation, and understanding the redemptive work of Christ.

The Communion is about His love. It is about His power to heal you and deliver you from every sickness and disease. And that is why our Lord Jesus wants us to partake of the holy Communion in *remembrance* of Him.

When the Jewish people use the word *remembrance*, it is not just a passive remembering or a sentimental recalling. It is a much stronger word that has the idea of *reenactment*, of going through the event again. It is about reenacting all He went through, seeing His body broken as you break the bread in your hands, and seeing His blood being shed for you as you drink of the cup. It is about actively valuing the cross, and seeing how powerful it is for you today as you remember it was for you that the King of kings suffered.

> THE COMMUNION
> IS ABOUT HIS
> LOVE AND
> HIS POWER
> TO HEAL AND
> DELIVER YOU.

FOCUS ON THE CROSS, NOT YOUR SICKNESS

Did you notice that our Lord Jesus told us to partake of the holy Communion in remembrance of Him, and not in remembrance of our medical conditions? There was a time when many of the children of Israel were dying from snakebites in the wilderness, and they cried out for Moses to pray that the Lord would take the serpents away. May I show you how God responded to the cry of the children of Israel?

> Then the LORD said to Moses, "Make a fiery serpent, and set it on a pole; and it shall be that everyone who is bitten, when he looks at it, shall live." (Num. 21:8)

God's response wasn't to take away the serpents. His response was to instruct Moses to make a replica of the very thing that was killing them—the serpent—and to set it on a pole for all to look at. The Bible goes on to tell us what happened next:

> So Moses made a bronze serpent, and put it on a pole; and so it was, if a serpent had bitten anyone, when he looked at the bronze serpent, he lived. (Num. 21:9)

The waves of nausea that immobilize you are real. The cramps that seize your body are real. The shortness of breath you have been struggling with is real. The pain that slices through your head with every move is real, just as the painful bites from the fiery serpents were real for the children of Israel. Right now, I pray that every pain and every discomfort be removed from your body in the mighty name of Jesus. Our Lord Jesus called healing "the children's bread" (Matt. 15:26). If you are a child of God, healing belongs to you.

IF YOU ARE A CHILD OF GOD, HEALING BELONGS TO YOU.

But my friend, your healing will not come from you focusing on your condition. Your healing will come as you do what the children of Israel did—they looked away from their wounds and looked at the bronze serpent lifted up on the pole.

Our Lord Jesus Himself spoke about this bronze serpent when He said, "And as Moses lifted up the serpent in the wilderness, even so must the Son of Man be lifted up" (John 3:14). The serpent on the pole is a picture of our Lord Jesus being lifted up on the cross, suspended between heaven and earth. He was rejected by man, and He was also rejected by God. His own Father had to turn away from Him because He was carrying all our sins.

But that's not all. It was a bronze serpent because bronze in the Bible speaks of judgment. God is holy and just, and God has to punish sin. God loved you and me so much that He sent Jesus to be our substitute, to bear our punishment and our judgment. At the cross, Jesus was punished for every sin. He bore every consequence and every curse of sin that you and I should have experienced, and that includes every sickness and every disease.

Even though many were killed by the snakebites, anyone among the children of Israel who *looked* at the bronze serpent was healed. The Hebrew word used for *look* in Numbers 21:9 is *nabat*, which means to "look intently at."[1] In the same way, when you partake of the holy Communion, don't partake with consciousness of the symptoms in your body. Partake of the holy Communion in remembrance of your

Lord Jesus and not in remembrance of your pain. Look to Him intently and with the expectation He will save you and heal you.

See Him lifted on the cross, being judged with your disease. If you have a problem with your kidney, see Jesus' kidney smitten with your disease at the cross. If you have a degenerative condition in your spine, see Jesus' spine smitten with that condition at the cross. When you see Jesus' body smitten with your disease, it cannot remain in you. Even if you have a "terminal" disease others have died from, look to Him and receive your healing!

Whenever you partake of the holy Communion, may I encourage you not to rush through it? The Lord loves you so much. Take some time to worship the Lord until you can sense His presence. Take time to magnify Him until your consciousness of His goodness and His healing virtue is so much greater than the feelings of your infirmity or the symptoms in your loved one's body. As you worship the person of our Lord Jesus, I

> **WHENEVER YOU PARTAKE OF THE COMMUNION, TAKE TIME TO WORSHIP AND MAGNIFY THE PERSON OF JESUS.**

believe you will receive all the benefits of the work that come with the person. That's why we partake in remembrance of Him.

SET APART FOR LIFE AND HEALTH

Some people are thrown off by the word *holy* when we talk about the holy Communion. To them, it feels antiquated and maybe even irrelevant. But did you know that to be "holy" simply means to be "set apart for God"[2] and to be *uncommon*? This speaks of the special nature of the Communion. Every time you partake of the holy Communion, you are allowing the Lord to set you apart from the world, and allowing Him to have a private time of intimacy and communion with you! Look at what God did for the children of Israel when the plagues came upon the land of Egypt. He declared:

"And in that day I will set apart the land of Goshen, in which My people dwell, that no swarms of flies shall be there, in order that you may know that I am the LORD in the midst of the land. I will make a difference between My people and your people." (Ex. 8:22–23)

In the same way, when you have divine insights on the power and significance of the holy Communion, the Lord Himself sets you apart and makes a difference between you and the people of the world. That means you are *not* like the people of the world. That means it may be common for the people of the world to catch the "common flu," or common for people in a particular age demographic to experience certain symptoms or to develop certain conditions. But you don't have to accept any "common" ailments because God has set you apart to be uncommon.

> YOU DON'T HAVE TO ACCEPT "COMMON" AILMENTS BECAUSE GOD HAS SET YOU APART.

In a world that is decaying and dying of illness, He has paid the price for you to be uncommonly healthy, whole, and healed. While the rest of the world can weaken with age, the Bible declares that "as your days, so shall your strength be" (Deut. 33:25), and that even as you advance in age, you can return to the days of your youth (Job 33:25). I pray that over you right now: as your days increase, may your strength and your health also increase, and may the Lord return the days of your youth to you, and cause your flesh to be young like a child's. Amen!

THE COMMUNION IS BASED ON REVELATION AND RELATIONSHIP

There is something about the holy Communion that you must know: simply ingesting the elements of the holy Communion will not yield results.

When I first started teaching our church about the Communion, some of my church members would simply tell their friends who fell sick to partake of the Communion. While I understood their intentions, just going through the motions of eating the bread and drinking the cup devoid of a *relationship* with our loving Savior does not work.

You can't just eat the elements out of superstition or with the attitude of simply "trying it out." You can't just put Communion elements in the hands of your loved ones who are sick and simply tell them to eat. Like I mentioned before, there is nothing magical about the elements of the Communion. If you have no revelation of the significance of the Communion, and no sense of His love in your heart, the holy Communion becomes empty. Unlike diets and fitness plans, which work if you follow the prescribed rules, the power of the holy Communion is based on a *revelation* of the redemptive work of Christ and faith in His finished work.

> **HE PAID THE PRICE FOR YOU TO BE UNCOMMONLY HEALTHY, WHOLE, AND HEALED.**

HOW TO INCREASE IN FAITH

If you don't have a revelation or you don't have faith, start listening to and watching sermons that are full of Jesus. Listen to teachings or read books about the holy Communion that unveil what He has done for you. The Bible tells us "faith comes by hearing, and hearing by the word of God" (Rom. 10:17). Did you notice that it doesn't say faith comes by "having heard"? If you don't have faith, you can cause faith to "come" by hearing and hearing. So keep on hearing, and don't be satisfied with simply having heard.

The New International Version translation of this verse also explains that faith comes by hearing "the word about Christ." Faith does not come by hearing about what you need to do to earn your blessing or how you have failed. It comes by hearing all about *Jesus* and His overwhelming love for you.

THE COMMUNION IS ABOUT INTIMATE FELLOWSHIP

Let me share with you something that I pray will cause your heart to be filled with such warmth as you see more and more of Jesus. The very word *communion* speaks of the relationship our Lord desires to have with us. The apostle Paul wrote:

> The cup of blessing which we bless, is it not the communion of the blood of Christ? The bread which we break, is it not the communion of the body of Christ? For we, though many, are one bread and one body; for we all partake of that one bread. Observe Israel after the flesh: Are not those who eat of the sacrifices partakers of the altar? (1 Cor. 10:16–18)

FAITH COMES BY HEARING ALL ABOUT JESUS AND HIS OVERWHELMING LOVE FOR YOU.

The word used for *communion* in the original Greek is the word *koinonia*, meaning "fellowship."[3] It also has the idea of an intimate participation, like the intimacy a husband and wife share when they say and do things no one else is privy to. Isn't that beautiful? Whenever you partake of the Communion, it's a time of intimacy between you and the Lord. It's a time you set aside to remember your heavenly Bridegroom, who loved you so much He gave Himself up for you (Eph. 5:25). It's a time you run to Him and lose yourself in His presence, and let His perfect love cast out every fear that may be eating at you.

He knows the secret fears of your heart as you look at the symptoms in your body. He knows the burdens that weigh you down as the doctors tell you about the long-term complications, side effects, and financial cost that treatment would entail. Run to Him, and cast all your anxieties, all your worries, and all your concerns on Him, for He cares about you with deepest affection, and watches over you very carefully (1 Peter 5:7 AMP).

As you take time to commune with Him and to remember Him through the holy Communion, do you know what happens? You become an "intimate participator" of the benefits of the body and the blood. Just as those who ate of the sacrifices become "partakers of the altar" (1 Cor. 10:18), when you eat the bread and drink the cup, you become a partaker of all Jesus accomplished at the cross. As you drink the cup, that is communion with and sharing in the blood of Christ (1 Cor. 10:16 NASB). As you take the broken bread, you are participating in the body of Christ that was broken for you (1 Cor. 10:16 NIV).

> **THE COMMUNION IS A TIME OF INTIMACY BETWEEN YOU AND THE LORD.**

EATING FRESH

When God provided manna for the children of Israel in the wilderness, Moses told the people, "Let no one leave any of it till morning" (Ex. 16:19). When some of them did not heed Moses' words and kept some till the next morning, it bred worms and stank. This reminds me of the law that the children of Israel had to observe when they brought the peace offering for thanksgiving: "The flesh of the sacrifice of his peace offering for thanksgiving shall be eaten the same day it is offered. *He shall not leave any of it until morning*" (Lev. 7:15).

These two verses speak of partaking fresh and not leaving the manna or the meat from the sacrifice to turn stale. In the same way, whenever we partake of the holy Communion, let's ask the Lord for a fresh revelation of what He did for us at the cross. Let's not ever become so familiar with the holy Communion that we start to see it as common and ordinary. We are holding the broken body of the Son of God and drinking of His shed blood.

Let me share with you another powerful passage of Scripture found in Hebrews 10:

> Therefore, brethren, having boldness to enter the Holiest by the blood of Jesus, *by a new and living way which He consecrated for us*, through the veil, that is, His flesh. (Heb. 10:19–20)

Through the cross, our Lord Jesus consecrated a "new and living way" for us to draw near to God not with fear and trepidation but with *boldness*. He allowed His own flesh to be torn so that we can have free access to our loving Father today. I want to draw your attention to the original Greek word used for *new* here. It is the word *prosphatos*, and it means "lately slaughtered, freshly killed."[4]

Why did the Holy Spirit use this unusual word here? Because whenever you partake of the holy Communion, God does not want you to partake as though you are commemorating a historical event that took place two thousand years ago. The cross transcends time. As you partake of the holy Communion in remembrance of Him, see your Lord Jesus before you, as though you are right there at Calvary. See your Lord Jesus *freshly slain*, bearing all your sicknesses and carrying all your pains. Don't partake ritualistically, but press in for a fresh revelation of His love that was demonstrated at the cross.

WHEN YOU EAT THE BREAD AND DRINK THE CUP, YOU BECOME A PARTAKER OF ALL THAT JESUS ACCOMPLISHED AT THE CROSS.

DELIVERED FROM DEEP DEPRESSION AFTER PARTAKING OF THE COMMUNION

Let me share with you the powerful testimony that Carey from Kentucky sent to me. I was touched as I read about how the Lord had ministered to Carey so personally, showing her that His provision of her healing was fresh every day:

I left an abusive marriage of twelve years, and my kids live with my ex-husband. I am only able to see them twice a year because I live twelve hours away.

After my last visit to see my kids last year, I fell into a deep depression. I couldn't get out of bed and slept up to twenty hours a day. Medications didn't help me. I lost fifty-eight pounds in five months because I couldn't eat.

Pastor Prince, I have been listening to your sermons on the holy Communion, literally for twenty-four hours on some days. I let them play as I sleep and listen for the few hours I am awake.

The revelation I received on the Communion has helped me step out of such deep darkness and depression. God showed me while I was standing in a line at Walmart waiting for my medication that His daily bread was my daily healing—for today, not yesterday or tomorrow, but today. Like with the manna that fell, if the children of Israel tried to keep it for the next day, it would spoil. Every day God provided new manna.

God told me it is the same with the Communion. That today He supplies all my healing through the elements of bread

> SEE THE LORD JESUS BEARING ALL YOUR SICKNESSES AND CARRYING ALL YOUR PAINS.

and juice, the simple things that represent what His Son did for me on the cross. And He said to me that when tomorrow comes, He will provide me with new bread and new healing for that day. So I began to take the Communion every day, and especially when I had really dark moments.

And here I stand, depression-free. God has restored hope in my life. Understanding the Communion better has given me hope and showed me that without Jesus hope is just an empty word.

All praise to God for His revelation! And thanks to people like you who never stray from preaching His truth.

Praise the Lord! I rejoice with Carey as she walks in freedom from the depression that had bound her, and I pray that whatever your diagnosis might be, you will also keep your eyes on your Lord Jesus and receive a fresh supply of His healing day by day.

Don't you love Jesus? Don't you find such assurance in knowing that your health and your healing are not based on rules concerning what you can eat or are forbidden to eat, but they are based on an intimate relationship with a living Savior? Don't you feel firmly established, knowing that He has done everything for you and your part is to simply look to Him and receive His finished work through the holy Communion? I have so much more I want to share with you that I know will bless you and fill your heart with faith to receive from Him.

> **OUR PART IS TO SIMPLY LOOK TO HIM AND RECEIVE HIS FINISHED WORK.**

But before we move on to the next chapter, may I encourage you to pause for a while?

Don't rush through this book. Don't walk away just having more information about what the holy Communion is about. Don't let this book speak only to your head. My prayer is that you will catch a revelation of Jesus that will cause your heart to burn within you (Luke 24:32).

Pause, and take time to worship the King of kings and the Lord of lords. Take time to sing to Him in psalms, hymns, and spiritual songs (Eph. 5:18–19). As you worship Him, He will release His fresh power over you to heal you, deliver you, and bring you the victory. Hallelujah. Praise the Lord for He is so good, His love endures forever!

8.

COMPLETELY COVERED, NO EXCLUSIONS

Thank you for staying with me all this way and giving me the privilege of sharing with you about a God who loves you so much He gave up His own Son to pay the price for your healing. By now you probably know much more about the holy Communion than you ever did before. You might also have learned some new Bible verses, and you may have found the testimonies and stories in this book inspiring.

But maybe you have been studying your insurance policy documents, and you realize they contain a list of exclusions and conditions. Or maybe you can't even get insurance coverage because of your pre-existing conditions, and you are wondering if God's healing power comes with its own set of exclusions as well. After all, what Jesus did at the cross happened more than two thousand years ago, when modern diseases such as Ebola and hypertension may not have existed. Would the holy Communion still apply to these?

In this chapter, I want to give you the assurance that there are *no exclusions* whatsoever in the finished work of Christ. Our Lord Jesus left nothing out when He bore our diseases on the cross. Its coverage is all-encompassing and perfectly comprehensive, and *every* condition has been covered! Please understand that I am all for you getting the necessary insurance coverage for you and your loved ones as I do for my family. Nevertheless, my faith and confidence will always be anchored to the unwavering power of the Lord.

> **JESUS LEFT NO SICKNESS OUT WHEN HE BORE OUR DISEASES ON THE CROSS.**

Perhaps you find it hard to believe that God is really so good. I do not know what you have gone through. Maybe you have been hurt by people in the church and that has colored your view of God. Maybe you feel all I have shared with you just seems too good to be true, and you find it hard to believe that this God I have written about would want to heal *you*.

Or maybe you have been disappointed before. You prayed so hard for a breakthrough, but it did not happen. You trusted in Him, or you had a loved one who did, but tragedy still took place. And now you don't want to believe because you *dare not* believe. You think it is better for you to just accept the doctor's diagnosis because there is no point in getting your hopes up. After all, medical science has already determined that your condition is incurable. Inoperable. Untreatable. Terminal. After all, your condition is very rare. After all, you have lived with this condition for so long.

My friend, the very fact you are reading this book tells me God *loves you* and He does *not* want you to give up!

Whatever health condition or disease you or your loved one is facing today, God can heal it. Even if you have received a very discouraging medical report and your chances of recovery are very slim in the natural, I pray that as we delve into God's Word today, you will find hope and strength. Don't give up just yet. Keep believing. Whatever medical science or doctors have said, the name of Jesus is higher and more powerful than any medical condition, disease, or sickness. Nothing is too hard for the Lord (Jer. 32:27).

HEALING FOR EVERY PART OF YOUR BODY

Earlier, I showed you God's instructions on how to partake of the Passover lamb, and I pray that the Holy Spirit has given you insights that have brought your appreciation of the holy Communion to a whole new level. But there is another powerful truth I want to highlight here:

> Then they shall eat the flesh on that night; roasted in fire, with unleavened bread and with bitter herbs they shall eat it. Do not eat it raw, nor boiled at all with water, but roasted in fire—*its head with its legs and its entrails.* (Ex. 12:8–9)

There are no insignificant details in the Bible. Why did God specifically mention that the lamb should be roasted in fire with its head, legs, and entrails? I believe He wants you to see that Jesus, your Passover Lamb, bore *every* condition in *every* part of your body. There is *no* disease, injury, or sickness He did not carry in His own body on the cross.

THERE IS *NO* DISEASE, INJURY, OR SICKNESS THAT HE DID NOT CARRY IN HIS OWN BODY ON THE CROSS.

The Israelites had lived under the stressful, cruel oppression of their slave masters and the horror of infanticide. Perhaps some of them suffered from post-traumatic stress disorder or had recurrent panic attacks. Perhaps some had chronic pain and physical disabilities from being brutally treated by their slave masters. It is not hard to imagine how they could also have succumbed to outbreaks and epidemics such as tuberculosis. But whatever condition they might have suffered from, I believe they were healed as they ate the roasted head, legs, and entrails of the lamb.

In the same way, God wants you and your loved ones healed of any condition that affects any part of your body. If you or a loved one has a neurological condition such as recurrent migraines, encephalitis, meningitis, dementia, or are suffering the effects of a stroke, see your Savior's brain afflicted with the condition on the cross as you partake of the Lord's Supper. Meditate on how He took upon Himself these infirmities so you can have perfect freedom from them (Matt. 8:17).

MOTHER FREED FROM ALZHEIMER'S AFTER PARTAKING OF THE COMMUNION

In chapter 5, I shared with you how Marcus was healed from Alzheimer's disease. Let me share with you another powerful testimony of healing from Alzheimer's disease that Paula from Texas sent to me:

My mother was ravaged by Alzheimer's disease. She was debilitated to the point that she did not recognize her family members. My father told me she was even beginning to wonder who he was at times.

GOD WANTS YOU HEALED OF ANY CONDITION THAT AFFECTS ANY PART OF YOUR BODY.

My parents live with me so I could see the daily moment-to-moment struggles and hardship. It was a miserable existence for her as well as for those of us trying to care for her. There were times I just missed my mom and wished to see her well again.

Then one day, my sister shared a praise report with me after following your teaching on the holy Communion, so I immediately began to partake of the Communion with my mother.

My mother went to bed on the third night after receiving the Communion and woke up the next day looking ten years younger. All the things she had forgotten how to do, she is doing again. She remembers who we all are now. She has stopped repeating herself, something she used to do from sun up to sun down, and is a complete joy to be around now. Jesus has healed her mind and set her free!

Praise Jesus for His finished work on the cross. We are still rejoicing that she is back. I have asked her about her experience and the best she could describe was that she was lost and trapped, but that's all over now.

I am so happy for my mom and our family. I am writing so others may have hope in the midst of what seems like a disease that offers no hope of recovery. Nothing is too big for the finished work of Christ Jesus and I praise Him for it. Now my mom will ask me if we are going to partake of the Communion, so I partake of it with her every day.

Thank you, Pastor Prince, for your teaching on the finished work of Christ Jesus. It has freed my mother!

> **GOD'S RESTORATION IS ALWAYS GREATER THAN THE ORIGINAL.**

To God be all the glory and all the praise! As you advance in years, don't accept the lie that you will become more forgetful. When the psalmist wrote that God "restores my soul" (Ps. 23:3), he used the word *nephesh* for *soul*. *Nephesh* includes your life, your emotions, and also your mind.[1] Even if you have experienced some degeneration in this area, the Lord can restore. And when the Lord restores, His restoration is always greater than the original in quality.

The world says that as your days increase and you age, your strength diminishes. But the Word declares, "As your days, so shall your strength be" (Deut. 33:25). Whose report will you believe? Keep partaking of the Lord's Supper and see yourself partaking of the mind of Christ. I declare that your mind is getting healthier and healthier in Jesus' name!

REDEEMED FROM STRESS AND STRESS-RELATED CONDITIONS

Before Jesus went through the scourging for our diseases, the Bible tells us He was under such duress in the Garden of Gethsemane that "His sweat became like great drops of blood falling down to the ground" (Luke 22:44). Medical science will tell you there is a rare condition called hematidrosis, where a person under extreme stress actually sweats blood.[2] I believe this is what happened to Jesus. He sweat great drops of blood from the brow of His head.

This is significant because of what happened in another garden, the garden of Eden. The Bible tells us that in that garden, Adam, the first man, sinned, and God said this to him:

> "Cursed is the ground because of you; through painful toil you will eat food from it all the days of your life. It will produce thorns and thistles for you, and you will eat the plants of the field. *By the sweat of your brow* you will eat your food." (Gen. 3:17–19 NIV)

Because of Adam's sin, the ground was cursed, resulting in Adam having to toil and sweat to get it to produce food. In other words, work became stressful for man. But when Jesus' sweat mingled with His redeeming blood, He delivered us from the curse of stress.

Thorns are also a picture of the cares of this world. When Jesus explained the parable of the sower, He referred to the thorns as the "cares of this world and the deceitfulness of riches" (Matt. 13:22). No wonder Jesus allowed the crown of thorns to be rammed

WHEN JESUS' SWEAT MINGLED WITH HIS REDEEMING BLOOD, HE DELIVERED US FROM THE CURSE OF STRESS.

onto His head. The next time you partake of the holy Communion, don't rush through it. See your Lord Jesus pierced not just by the nails but also by the thorns.

It was all for you. It was all for your freedom. The children of Israel were set free from physical chains and shackles. Today I declare to you in Jesus' name that you are loosed from the chains of stress and any stress-induced condition.

Stress can cause cardiovascular diseases, eating disorders, menstrual issues, sexual dysfunctions, gastrointestinal problems, as well as skin and hair problems. If you are facing challenges in any of these areas today, His blood has redeemed you, and His blood has saved you. May you walk in the fullness of all He died to give you.

HEALING FOR EYE, NOSE, THROAT, EAR, AND MOUTH CONDITIONS

Don't forget that your eyes, nose, throat, ears, and mouth are all situated in your head. If you have a condition in any of these areas, see your affected organ in Jesus' body on the cross. For instance, if you have been diagnosed with eye conditions such as glaucoma, cataracts, or ocular hypertension, see Jesus' eyes stricken with those conditions while He hung on the cross, and receive His perfect and healthy eyes.

HEALING FOR YOUR LIMBS

Do you have any affliction that causes you to be weak in your legs or affects your mobility? Whether the pain or condition is due to an accident, degeneration, or injury, God wants to set you free from it.

As you partake of the Lord's Supper, see yourself eating the roasted legs of the Lamb and receive strength. See Jesus taking every muscle, knee, or ankle condition for you, and see His feet nailed to the cross so that yours can be free to go wherever you want.

HEALING FOR INTERNAL ORGANS

God also told the Israelites to feed on the roasted entrails of the lamb. By now you probably know why—so that *their* entrails could be completely well.

The entrails refer to all your internal organs, and that includes your stomach, bowels, heart, kidneys, liver, prostate, and reproductive organs. Whatever condition you might have, whether it is irritable bowel syndrome, an ulcerated stomach, cirrhosis, chronic lower respiratory disease, or pneumonia, see Jesus on the cross smitten with your disease and receive His perfect health in these areas.

HEALING FOR EVERY AFFLICTION

Whatever affliction you might have in any part of your body, I want you to know every condition has been borne by Jesus on the cross. While God specifically instructed the children of Israel to eat the Passover lamb's head with its legs and entrails, the *whole* lamb was roasted. This means no matter what disease you are battling today, Jesus has taken it on Himself.

> SEE JESUS ON THE CROSS SMITTEN WITH YOUR DISEASE AND RECEIVE HIS PERFECT HEALTH.

Your part is to keep partaking of the channel of divine health He has given you until you see the manifestation of your victory. Your part is to lift up your hands to Him and say, "Lord Jesus, I receive Your healing. By the stripes that fell on You, every part of my body—every cell, every organ—is healed and functions at peak efficiency. Thank You, Jesus, for Your healing."

REDEEMED FROM THE CURSE OF THE LAW

I pray that you have caught a glimpse of the absolute perfection of His finished work on the cross, and how much He loves you to have borne every imaginable disease upon His own body so you need *not* suffer them.

But I am not done showing you how you can turn to the cross for *any* and *every* medical challenge and condition. The Bible tells us that our Lord Jesus redeemed us from *every* curse of the law so that the blessing of Abraham might come upon us:

> Christ has redeemed us from the curse of the law, having become a curse for us (for it is written, "Cursed is everyone who hangs on a tree"), that the blessing of Abraham might come upon the Gentiles in Christ Jesus, that we might receive the promise of the Spirit through faith. (Gal. 3:13–14)

Deuteronomy 28 has a very long and detailed list of curses. I asked the Lord why He took so much time to elucidate the details of the curses, and He showed me it was so that after Jesus died on the cross, we would know what He redeemed us from. Once I saw that, reading about the curses became a blessing for me because it reminds me that we have been redeemed from *every single one* of the curses.

It would not be possible for us to go through all the curses, but I want to focus on the curses that cover sicknesses and diseases. Let me show you exactly what Jesus has redeemed you and me from:

- Consumption (diseases that cause your lungs to waste away), fever, and inflammation (Deut. 28:22)
- Boils, tumors, scurvy, "the itch, from which you cannot be cured" (Deut. 28:27 NLT)

- Madness, blindness, and panic (Deut. 28:28 NLT)
- Severe boils that cannot be healed (Deut. 28:35)
- Great and prolonged plagues, and serious and prolonged sicknesses (Deut. 28:59)

Wow. Aren't you glad Christ has redeemed you from the curse of the law? He has redeemed you from all the diseases and afflictions mentioned in Deuteronomy 28. And if you think your particular condition is not quite covered, the Bible goes on to mention "all the diseases of Egypt" (Deut. 28:60). Egypt is a picture of the world. As the people of God, we do not have to be afraid of the diseases the world suffers because He has brought us out of the world, and now we may be *in* the world but we are not *of* this world (John 17:11, 14).

Not only that.

It also goes on to include "every sickness and every plague, which is not written in this Book of the Law" (Deut. 28:61).

Hallelujah! Can you see that *every* disease and *every* condition is part of the curse of the law and that Christ has redeemed us from *every* curse? God wants you so blessed in your health that just as He put all your sins on Jesus' body, He also put all your diseases on Jesus' body. God loves you so much He allowed His own Son to *become a curse* so you can be redeemed from the curse of the law.

That doesn't mean the enemy won't try to enforce symptoms of the curse in your life. But whenever the enemy tries to bring on a symptom of the curse, you can reject it. Refuse to accept it. You have already been redeemed from that symptom in Jesus' name!

GOD CAN MAKE A WAY

I may not understand fully the circumstances you are going through or the depths of your despair as you watch your loved one fighting to stay alive. What I know is this: God loves *you* more than you can ever comprehend, and He *can* make a way even when there seems to be no way.

Exodus 14 records how the children of Israel thought they were doomed when the mighty Egyptian army closed in on them. It appeared that death was inevitable. They would either be slaughtered by the Egyptians or perish in the watery grave of the Red Sea. But I want you to see what Moses said to them:

> And Moses said to the people, "Do not be afraid. Stand still, and see the salvation of the LORD, which He will accomplish for you today. *For the Egyptians whom you see today, you shall see again no more forever.* The LORD will fight for you, and you shall hold your peace." (Ex. 14:13–14)

Then God split open the sea, and the children of Israel "walked on dry land in the midst of the sea" (Ex. 14:29). But God didn't stop there. God caused the sea to return to its full depth while Pharaoh's formidable forces were still in pursuit, and I love how the Bible spells this out: "Not so much as one of them remained" (Ex. 14:28).

WHEN THE ENEMY TRIES TO BRING ON A SYMPTOM OF THE CURSE, REFUSE TO ACCEPT IT.

Beloved, you or your loved one might be faced with a daunting and seemingly impossible medical situation. All your fretting and tears cannot change your situation, but there is One who can. Do not be afraid. Stand still and see the salvation of the Lord. *He* will fight for you. *He* will overcome your enemies for you. Don't keep asking *why* you have the disease. Don't accept the disease or believe the lie that you deserve to be sick because of the wrong you have done. The Lord Jesus has *already* paid the price for your wholeness. Just put your hand in His and let Him lead you through your situation.

He will cause you to walk on dry land in the midst of the sea. The negative reports, medical statistics, and symptoms that you see may spell an inescapable situation, but He *will* make a way that will stun everyone around you. The Red Sea you thought would drown you will become the burial ground for your enemies instead. You might see them today, but you shall see those oppressive symptoms *no more forever*!

> STAND STILL AND SEE THE SALVATION OF THE LORD. HE WILL FIGHT FOR YOU.

I see your migraine headaches gone. The inflammation in your joints gone. The paralyzing fatigue gone. The negative report about your unborn baby gone. The blood in your urine gone. Not so much as one of them will remain!

Even when experts have said that you have only months or even days to live, God can make a way. In the face of death, lift up the elements of the holy Communion and proclaim that His blood gives you life. His blood gives you forgiveness of sins. Even if doctors have tried everything they know and your loved one is still not responding, the Lord can make a way. Even if you have been a slave to endless rounds of treatment and medication for as long as you can remember, He can make a way!

HEALED OF MENIERE'S DISEASE

One of my leaders shared with me how doctors diagnosed him with Meniere's disease when he suddenly suffered bouts of intense vertigo that completely incapacitated him for hours. He did not know what triggered them, but whenever a vertigo attack occurred, waves of nausea would overtake him, and he would find himself throwing up uncontrollably. He would also experience symptoms of tinnitus regularly, where every sound around him became magnified or distorted, and he would not be able to hear what people were saying to him.

Needless to say, it was terrifying for him because the attacks were sudden and unpredictable and could happen while he was driving. His doctors told him that his condition was genetic, as his mum had also been diagnosed with Meniere's disease some years earlier. He was told that while they could prescribe medication to manage the symptoms, there was no cure for his condition. They warned him the symptoms were, in fact, likely to get even worse.

In the meantime, each time he suffered an attack, he would be slumped over the toilet bowl, retching and vomiting until he was exhausted. It felt like he was trapped in the churning waters of a violent storm from which he could not escape.

Then one day, as he spent time in the Word of God, the Lord led him to this passage:

> "Behold, all those who were incensed against you shall be ashamed and disgraced; they shall be as nothing, and those who strive with you shall perish. *You shall seek them and not find them*—those who contended with you. *Those who war against you shall be as nothing, as a nonexistent thing.* For I, the LORD your God, will hold your right hand, saying to you, 'Fear not, I will help you.'" (Isa. 41:11–13)

He said, "When God gave me that word, I kept meditating on it and kept it in my spirit. The words 'shall be as a nonexistent thing' kept jumping out at me, and I *knew* that I had it. I was healed."

He did not see the full manifestation of his healing immediately, but he had faith he was already healed *because of the word he received*. Faith is the substance of things hoped for, "the evidence of things not seen" (Heb. 11:1). So even before he saw the reality, he *knew* he was healed.

He continued to partake of the holy Communion regularly, but he no longer did so out of any sense of fear the symptoms would become increasingly debilitating. Instead, he partook knowing he was *already* healed, and after some time, he "stopped experiencing the symptoms altogether." Right now, as I write this, he has been completely symptom-free for more than a year. All glory to our lovely Savior!

What a powerful passage to meditate on if you are faced with the enemies of sickness and disease today. Doesn't it remind you of what the Lord did for the children of Israel when He split open the Red Sea for them even though it appeared like all was lost? The Lord is no respecter of persons. Put your trust in Him. He can make a way when there seems to be no way. If He did it for the children of Israel, and He did it for the brother in my church, He can do it for you too.

> **HE CAN MAKE A WAY WHEN THERE SEEMS TO BE NO WAY.**

GOD'S WORD BRINGS LIFE AND HEALING TO YOUR WHOLE BODY

In the testimony we just read, I love it that even before the brother stopped experiencing symptoms in his body, he had faith he was already healed *because of the word he received.* I am sure it was not always easy to believe he was healed, especially during times when he found himself throwing up uncontrollably. But he fought every battle of fear and unbelief armed with that verse from the Lord, and that is what I want to encourage you to do too. Find promises from the Lord for you in the Scriptures and hold on to them.

AS JESUS IS, SO ARE YOU IN THIS WORLD

I have received many other healing testimonies where precious individuals were healed as they clung to specific promises in His Word for them. Some years ago, I preached on 1 John 4:17, which says, "As He is, so are we in this world." Our Lord Jesus bore our sins and our diseases in His own body on the cross, and He rose from the grave *without them*. This means that as Jesus is without any disease, and as He is in complete divine health, so are we in this world. As He is crowned with glory and honor, so are we in this world.

There was a lady in my church who heard my message. That week she had to go for a mammogram. When the medical report came back, it showed that there was a lump in her breast. Her doctors were concerned and told her to come back in the evening so they could draw some samples from her to conduct a biopsy.

Do you know what she did?

She wrote on her medical report, "As Jesus is, so am I in this world. Lord Jesus, do You have lumps in Your breast?"

I saw her report for myself with those words written across the top of it. And then she prayed, "Lord, as You are, and You are free from lumps, *so am I* in this world." That's all. It was just a simple prayer.

When she went back that evening, the doctors checked her, and they rechecked her, and they checked her again. But they could not find *any* lump!

The doctors were baffled and could not explain how the lump could have simply disappeared. We don't need to know how; we just need to know *who*. It was our Jesus who healed her. Hallelujah!

The amazing thing is, I have received testimonies from so many other precious individuals who were encouraged by this lady's praise report. They stood on this same scripture and kept confessing it over themselves until they received their breakthroughs.

OVERCOME THE ENEMY BY THE WORD OF OUR TESTIMONY

I really believe many others received their own miracle after reading this lady's praise report because reading testimonies is God's way. This is why the Bible is filled with so many healing testimonies. The Holy

Spirit recorded story after story of healings, many of them in great detail, for our benefit.

There is no healing too big or too small for the Lord. Testimonies from Peter's mother-in-law who was healed of fever (Matt. 8:14–15), to the man whose withered hand became as healthy and normal as his other hand (Matt. 12:9–13), to the woman who had been bent over for eighteen years and could not stand up straight (Luke 13:11–13) were all recorded for

> **THERE IS NO HEALING TOO BIG OR TOO SMALL FOR THE LORD.**

us. There are praise reports of blind eyes healed (John 9:1–7; Mark 8:22–25; Luke 18:35–43; Matt. 9:27–30), deaf ears opened (Mark 7:32–35), and the mute speaking (Matt. 9:32–33). There are testimonies of those who had died being brought back to life (John 11:1–44; Mark 5:35–42).

Healing accounts are also recorded in the Old Testament. Naaman was healed of leprosy (2 Kings 5:1–14). Hezekiah had a terminal illness and was told he would not recover and would die, but God healed him and extended his life by fifteen years (2 Kings 20:1–7). And these are just a few of the many testimonies recorded for us in the Word of God.

TESTIMONIES OF HEALINGS AFTER PARTAKING OF THE HOLY COMMUNION

Over the years, I have received countless testimonies from people who were healed as they kept partaking of the holy Communion by faith. Someone wrote to share how her father, who had been in the intensive care unit, was pulled back from the brink of death. She gave a detailed account of how her father improved each time they partook of the holy Communion on his behalf. It started with his kidney functions being partially restored, then his heart rate and blood pressure stabilized, and then he was able to breathe independently. Finally, he was discharged and was able to celebrate his eighty-sixth birthday at his favorite restaurant. Even his physician admitted his recovery was a miracle.

Several testimonies came in from people who were healed of cancer. A brother who developed inflammation of the brain and was given a very low chance of surviving was healed. Someone else testified of how she delivered a healthy baby without Down syndrome despite receiving reports that her baby would have this genetic disorder. Another person who had dealt with constant pain after breaking her hip was healed. A baby who was born ten weeks premature and struggled with multiple health problems was healed. There were those who were healed of severe anxiety attacks, deep depression, and sleep disorders. There were testimonies from people healed of lupus, asthma, skin conditions, tumors, gastric pains, and many other conditions.

My friend, Jesus is the same yesterday, today, and forever, and He continues to heal today.

It doesn't matter what your medical challenge is today. He can heal you. The holy Communion is not a gimmick; it is not a ritual; it is not a sentimental custom. It is the greatest expression of God's love. When you partake of the bread with

HIS EARS ARE ATTENTIVE TO YOUR SOFTEST SIGH.

this revelation, you release your faith to receive His health and wholeness in exchange for your sicknesses and diseases. When you drink the cup, you are reminded that the blood of the sinless Son of God didn't just bring you forgiveness, but it also made you eternally righteous, holy, and blameless. So today, because of the Lord's body that was broken and His blood that was shed, you have perfect standing before the Father, and His ears are attentive to your softest sigh.

In this book I can share only a small sample of the testimonies, but there are so many more praise reports you can draw encouragement from. My team has prepared a website where you can read the testimonies for yourself. If you are believing for a breakthrough, please go to JosephPrince.com/eat and take some time to read the praise reports.

And when you receive your breakthrough, please write to me using the form at JosephPrince.com/eat so we can continue adding to the testimonies there.

Whatever you might be facing today, my heart is that the testimonies recounted here will deposit faith in you, even if it is just a speck. Our Lord Jesus told His disciples that if they had faith like a mustard seed, nothing would be impossible for them (Matt. 17:20). Do you know how small a mustard seed is? It is quite literally a tiny speck. And that's all you need!

> THE MORE YOU READ TESTIMONIES OF HIS GOODNESS AND FAITHFULNESS, THE MORE FAITH FOR YOUR HEALING WILL COME.

Maybe you don't have faith to believe the medical condition in your body will disappear immediately. But can you have faith to believe He really loves you? That He really is as good as the Word says He is? Then let's start with that. I believe the more you read testimonies of His goodness and faithfulness and the more you immerse yourself in hearing all about Jesus and His finished work, the more faith for your healing will come.

I am looking forward to receiving your praise report. Together, let's ignite the faith of others who are still believing for their breakthroughs. David used the same sword that Goliath tried to use against him to cut off Goliath's head. As you share your testimony, that's what you will be doing. You will be allowing the Lord to use what the devil meant for evil against you and to turn it around for good and His glory. You will be helping others overcome the enemy through the word of your testimony (Rev. 12:11).

9.

DON'T GIVE UP!

I hope you have had the chance to read some of the testimonies in the URL I shared with you in the last chapter. Aren't you glad we have a God of miracles and that He continues to heal, save, and deliver today?

But maybe you have been partaking of the holy Communion for some time, yet nothing seems to be happening. Maybe you are tired of hearing about the testimonies of others because you can't help but think, *How about me, Lord? Have You forgotten about me? When am I going to receive my healing? How long do I have to wait?*

Beloved, I want you to know it is okay for you to cry out to the Lord and to ask, "How long, Lord?"

That's what the psalmist David did, and we get to read the words he poured out to the Lord in his anguish:

> IT IS OKAY FOR YOU TO CRY OUT TO THE LORD AND TO ASK, "HOW LONG, LORD?"

How long, O LORD? Will You forget me forever?
How long will You hide Your face from me?
How long shall I take counsel in my soul,

Having sorrow in my heart daily?
How long will my enemy be exalted over me? (Ps. 13:1–2)

God loves you and He cares for you. He knows the discouragement that overwhelms you when it feels like the enemy of sickness has had the upper hand over you for so long and God feels so far away. He isn't shocked when you express such thoughts. He wants you to run to Him even when you have such thoughts. He knows exactly what you are going through and the despair that seems to be crushing you. Just bring it all to the Lord, but don't stay in that place of discouragement.

Continue reading what David wrote. Psalm 13 ends with this:

> **BRING ALL YOUR DESPAIR TO THE LORD, BUT DON'T STAY IN THAT PLACE OF DISCOURAGEMENT.**

But I have trusted in Your mercy;
My heart shall rejoice in Your salvation.
I will sing to the LORD,
Because He has dealt bountifully with me. (Ps. 13:5–6)

But.

One little word that makes all the difference.

It may feel like hopelessness might overcome you, *but* don't give up. In the original Hebrew, the word the psalmist David used for *mercy* is *hesed* (grace), while the word used for *salvation* is *yeshua*. Keep trusting in His grace. Keep your eyes on your *Yeshua*, your Jesus. Your salvation—welfare, deliverance, and victory—is found in Him!

As you talk to the Lord and spend time in His presence, you will find He does not give you the answer; He *is* the answer. Even when your outward circumstances do not seem to change, you will find that *you* have changed. Look at what happened to David as he cried out to God in Psalm 3:

LORD, how they have increased who trouble me!
Many are they who rise up against me.
Many are they who say of me,
"There is no help for him in God." *Selah*

But You, O LORD, are a shield for me,
My glory and the One who lifts up my head. (Ps. 3:1–3)

Did you notice the *selah* in the psalm? You will find such *"selah* moments" throughout David's psalms. That means David paused . . . and listened.

In those moments, David turned his eyes from his troubles and looked to his God. In those moments, I believe he remembered afresh that he did not have to fight his battles for the Lord of hosts fought for him (1 Sam. 17:45–47). He remembered afresh the God who had delivered him from the paw of the lion and the paw of the bear, the God who overcame Goliath without sword or spear. And as he looked to the Lord, he strengthened himself in the Lord (1 Sam. 30:6), and that's when things started to change.

Change came when he shifted his focus away from his painful and dire circumstances and allowed himself to be absorbed instead in the *grace* of the Lord, when he paused and tuned in to what the Lord was encouraging him with on the inside.

I believe that in those few moments of meditating on God's goodness and mercy, he heard the Lord say to him, "David, why are you worried about all these people coming against you? *I* am your shield. *I* am the glory and the lifter of your head." That was what brought about David's turning point in the situation. God's comfort came to David as he chose to *selah*.

RUN TO THE LORD IN THE PRESENCE OF YOUR ENEMIES.

Does it seem like your enemies have increased and many are rising up against you? Have you been getting one bad report after another from the doctor? Maybe you were admitted to the hospital for a particular condition. But as the doctors examined you, they found more to be concerned about, things you weren't even aware of previously. And now your heart is heavy because it feels like maybe even God can't help you.

At times like this, do what David did.

Selah.

Pause and choose to run to the Lord in the presence of your enemies.

When David came back to the psalm, his enemies were still there. But he could rise up and declare, "But You, O LORD, are a shield for me, my glory and the One who lifts up my head."

In your *selah* moments with the Lord, you will find your turning point and victory. Don't remain discouraged. Don't run away from Him. Run *to* Him and worship Him.

And if you don't know where to start, may I invite you to join us? As a church we had a powerful, intimate, and liberating time worshiping with the psalms of David

> EXALT HIM INSTEAD OF MAGNIFYING YOUR CHALLENGES, AND WATCH HIM BRING VICTORY TO YOUR SITUATION!

some time ago, and we would love for you to experience it too. You can do so by going to JosephPrince.com/eat. Exalt Him and His *hesed* instead of magnifying your challenges, and watch Him bring victory to your situation!

YOUR HEALING CAN TAKE PLACE INSTANTANEOUSLY

You can receive healing through the prayer of faith (Mark 11:24), and many times during our services, people were instantaneously healed as the gifts of healings flowed (1 Cor. 12:9).

I love it when God pours out the gifts of the Holy Spirit. When He pours, He doesn't pour from a jar or even a barrel. It feels like all of heaven is being poured out on us, and no matter how big our auditorium is and how many other service venues we have, we still cannot contain all the good God has for us.

There is something powerful about being in church when the name of our Lord Jesus is lifted up. There is a corporate anointing at work when the church gathers together because Jesus said, "For where two or three are gathered together in My name, I am there in the midst of them" (Matt. 18:20).

Where Jesus is, death turns into life and resurrection, weakness becomes strength, little becomes much, and in the presence of the Lord is fullness of joy and pleasures forevermore (Ps. 16:11). In His presence, you will experience resurrection and life (John 11:25). That's why the Bible tells us not to forsake the assembling of ourselves together (Heb. 10:25). When we gather, He is in the midst of us.

LITTLE BY LITTLE HE WILL DRIVE OUT YOUR ENEMIES

I would love for everyone to receive immediate and complete healing all the time. But while we know miracles of instant healing can happen, may I tell you that you don't have to have an instantaneous manifestation or feel something tangibly happening in your body to know God is healing you? The moment you partake of the holy Communion in faith, your healing has begun. Don't be discouraged if you don't receive an instantaneous manifestation of your healing.

> THE MOMENT YOU PARTAKE OF THE HOLY COMMUNION IN FAITH, YOUR HEALING HAS BEGUN.

Most people who have sent in their healing testimonies to my ministry weren't healed in a spectacular prayer meeting or when a man or woman of God laid hands on them. They were healed gradually by the

Lord as they partook of the channel through which He ordained for us to receive His supernatural life and health—the holy Communion.

In chapter 1, I shared with you how the apostle Paul had highlighted the reason many in the church were weak and sick. The reason he gave wasn't "not enough laying of hands on the sick" or "not holding enough healing rallies." The reason he gave was "not discerning the Lord's body" (1 Cor. 11:29–30).

Sometimes teachings on the prayer of faith can put pressure on you to believe you have complete healing the moment you pray. But truth be told, most of us don't have that kind of faith. As for the gifts of healings, they operate as the Spirit wills (1 Cor. 12:11) and not as man wills. When it comes to the holy Communion, there is no pressure. Each time you partake in faith, you receive a measure of healing. Each time you partake, you get better and better.

> **EACH TIME YOU PARTAKE OF THE COMMUNION IN FAITH, YOU RECEIVE A MEASURE OF HEALING.**

Sometimes we get impatient and we want the Lord to drive out all our enemies at once. May I show you a passage that I pray will encourage you? This is what the Lord said to the children of Israel as they were preparing to enter the promised land:

> "I will not drive them out from before you in one year, lest the land become desolate and the beasts of the field become too numerous for you. Little by little I will drive them out from before you, until you have increased, and you inherit the land." (Ex. 23:29–30)

Little by little.

Little by little.

Today we don't face the Hivites, Hittites, or Canaanites like the children of Israel did. But our enemies might be renal failure, leukemia, or high blood pressure.

Whatever it is, don't be discouraged. The symptoms might still be there even though you have partaken of the holy Communion, but keep partaking. The manifestation of your healing is coming. The enemy is being driven out from your life. Your healing might not be taking place as quickly as you would like it to, but it *is* taking place. My friend, don't give up!

SUPERNATURAL BUT UNSPECTACULAR HEALING THROUGH THE HOLY COMMUNION

YOUR HEALING IS TAKING PLACE. DON'T GIVE UP!

Even when it comes to the Communion, there are times when someone partakes of the Lord's Supper and the healing that follows is immediate. But this is usually the exception rather than the rule. In most instances, what I have seen is that healing takes place gradually. Gradual does not mean healing is not happening.

Some years ago, I had a condition in my tailbone that lasted for some time. I suffered a sharp pain each time I got up after sitting down, even if the chair was soft and cushioned. When I consulted a doctor, he told me it was wear and tear "due to age" and there was nothing I could do about it. When he said that, I realized my body was succumbing to the natural forces of aging.

But I refused to accept it because I am in this world but not of this world (John 17:11, 14). I *should not* be subject to what the world suffers. And neither should you. As we saw in chapter 8, Christ has redeemed us from the curse of the law and that includes all the diseases the world suffers.

I decided to avail myself of the Lord's provision and started partaking of the holy Communion for my tailbone pain.

Do you know what happened immediately after I partook of the holy Communion?

I got up from my seat.

And intense pain shot through my body.

The next day, I partook of the Lord's Supper again. When I stood up, the pain jolted me once again; and again, I had to pause for a moment before I could walk.

This went on for some time. I would partake of the holy Communion, but the pain would remain.

Then one day, I suddenly realized I had stood up without flinching. In fact, when I thought about it, I realized I hadn't suffered any pain for a few days. I was healed!

I don't know how long I had been partaking of the holy Communion for my tailbone pain. I didn't even realize it when I was healed. The Lord had healed me supernaturally. But the healing took place so gradually, as I kept partaking of the Lord's Supper, that I did not immediately realize when I was healed. I believe that is how most healings take place.

> EVERYTHING YOU NEED FROM GOD HAS ALREADY BEEN SUPPLIED TO YOU THROUGH THE CROSS.

PARTAKE OF THE HOLY COMMUNION OFTEN

This is why our Lord Jesus said, "This do, as often as you drink it, in remembrance of Me" (1 Cor. 11:25). Notice He said "as often" and not "as rarely" or "as infrequently."

That tells us He was referring to constantly partaking of the holy Communion. But how do we define "often"? The Lord leaves it to us to decide.

I just know this: the early church partook of the Communion *daily*, breaking bread from house to house (Acts 2:46). They must have had a revelation of how beneficial the Communion was to their bodies and were partaking of the Communion as often as they could. I am not saying we have to partake of the holy Communion every day. But if you feel led to, then please do so by all means.

VICTORY IS ALREADY YOURS

So what should you do when you continue to be confronted with the symptoms or even when the enemy keeps reminding you of so-and-so who wasn't healed?

Keep on partaking of the holy Communion and thanking the Lord for the healing He has given you. Everything you need from God has already been supplied to you through the cross. Scripture tells us He has *already* redeemed you from the curse of the law and from every sickness and disease (Gal. 3:13).

When Jesus cursed the fig tree, it didn't look dead immediately. But by the next day, the disciples saw it had dried up from its roots (Mark 11:12–14, 20–21). In the same way, you might still see the symptoms after you have partaken of the Communion. But that sickness has already died at its roots the moment you received His finished work, so your part is to rest in what Christ has done.

YOUR PART IS TO REST IN WHAT CHRIST HAS DONE.

When our Lord Jesus instituted the holy Communion, He took the cup and gave thanks (Matt. 26:27). The Greek word for gave thanks is *eucharisteo*, which means "to express gratitude."[1] This is why the holy Communion is also known as the Eucharist. You give thanks for something that is already done, that you have already received. So even if the symptoms are still in your body, you can give thanks and call yourself healed because His Word declares that "by His stripes we are healed" (Isa. 53:5).

Don't try to "get" healing for yourself or your loved one. It is already yours! The enemy has already been conquered (Col. 2:15).

Jesus has *already* given you divine health and wholeness. Always remember this: as a believer, you do not fight for victory; you fight *from* victory.

DO NOT CONSIDER YOUR OWN BODY

My friend, let's be like Abraham, who was convinced God was able to do what He had promised. Even though Abraham was very advanced in years, he believed God's promise that He would make him a father of many nations and *did not consider his own body* or the deadness of his wife Sarah's womb (Rom 4:19).

And you know the story: Isaac was born to Abraham when he was already one hundred years old (Gen. 21:5) and when Sarah was about ninety. In the natural, that was impossible as they were both past the natural childbearing age.

But Abraham did not consider the deadness of his own body; he considered God's promise. Romans 4:20–21 tells us he "did not waver at the promise of God through unbelief, but was strengthened in faith, giving glory to God, and being fully convinced that what He had promised He was also able to perform."

> AS A BELIEVER, YOU DO NOT FIGHT FOR VICTORY; YOU FIGHT *FROM* VICTORY.

In the same way, even if there is a sickness in your body, may I encourage you to be like Abraham? *Do not consider* the symptoms in your body or the bad report given by your doctor. Instead, fix your eyes on our Lord Jesus, and consider the promise in God's Word, which declares that by Jesus' stripes you are healed. Keep partaking of the Communion in faith, thanking Him that His body was broken so yours might be whole. And as you partake, like the children of Israel, get ready for and keep expecting your physical deliverance.

WHAT TO DO WHEN YOU HAVE NO FAITH

But what if you are at a place where you feel like you can't conjure up any more faith, let alone "not waver at the promise of God" like Abraham?

What if you are thinking, *Pastor Prince, I want to believe all you have shared. I really do. But I have tried and it does not look like anything is happening. It's been so long. I'm really tired of trying. I have no more faith to carry on.*

Let me show you what the Bible says about Sarah:

> By faith Sarah herself also received strength to conceive seed, and she bore a child when she was past the age, *because she judged Him faithful who had promised.* (Heb. 11:11)

There was faith involved when Sarah conceived and bore a child. But if you think faith is awfully hard and that you simply have no faith, I pray this will encourage you.

BELIEVE THE PROMISE IN GOD'S WORD THAT BY JESUS' STRIPES YOU ARE HEALED.

How did Sarah receive her miracle after so long and when it seemed impossible in the natural? She "judged Him faithful who had promised."

It seems so simple, but therein lay her miracle. The faith walk isn't hard. It is easy and effortless. When your faith runs out, judge God faithful. When you do not know how to have faith anymore, reckon on *His* faithfulness. Even when it seems you don't have faith, remember that *He* is faithful. Lean on *His* faithfulness.

Don't give up because you think you don't have enough faith. Once God gives you a promise, it is not for you to conjure up faith. It is for you to rest in the One who promised, knowing that He is faithful.

There is a beautiful verse I want you to emblazon across your spirit and memorize if possible. It is a verse that will steady you in the fight of faith when it seems like your answers are not forthcoming:

If we are faithless, He remains faithful; He cannot deny Himself.
(2 Tim. 2:13)

Even when you are faithless, He remains faithful. At the cross, as Jesus carried all our sins, God the Father had to turn away from His Son, and Jesus cried out, "My God, My God, why have You forsaken Me?" (Matt. 27:46). He paid the price for you and me to have God's constant presence, and because of that, God will never leave you nor forsake you (Heb. 13:5). He will never relax His hold on you. When you feel faithless, know that you don't have to try to hold on to Him—He is the One holding on to you. The Bible says the Lord your God holds your right hand, saying to you, "Fear not, I will help you" (Isa. 41:13).

If you are feeling weak today, do not worry and fear not. You can rest in His arms of love, knowing He will take care of you.

Don't look at your own faith and think, *I don't have enough faith for the breakthrough I need.* Faith is nothing more than looking to Jesus. There were only two individuals in the Gospels whom Jesus described as having "great faith": the centurion who believed Jesus only had to speak a word and his servant at home would be healed (Matt. 8:5–13) and the Syro-Phoenician woman to whom Jesus said, "O woman, great is your faith!" (Matt. 15:21–28).

FAITH IS NOTHING MORE THAN LOOKING TO JESUS.

And neither of them was conscious of their own faith.

Do you want to know what they were conscious of? They were conscious of Jesus. They saw Him as the One who was faithful and powerful. They had a great estimation of His grace and goodness. And as they saw Him in His grace, He saw them in their faith!

Don't worry about whether you have enough faith or not. Just look to Jesus. Spend time in His presence. Watch or listen to sermons that are full of Jesus. When you touch Jesus, you touch faith because He is the author and finisher of faith (Heb. 12:2). The Bible declares He is faithful, and He will not allow you to go through more than what you can bear (1 Cor. 10:13). He *will* carry you through.

When your battle with your sickness has been so long-drawn, and you feel utterly depleted and have no more strength to even have faith, may I encourage you to do this? Take time to go into the Lord's presence and just tell Him:

> **THE BIBLE DECLARES THAT HE IS FAITHFUL, AND HE WILL CARRY YOU THROUGH.**

Lord Jesus, thank You for Your faithfulness to me. You are faithful in Your goodness to me. You are faithful to carry out Your promises in my life. You are faithful to see what is happening to me, and You are faithful to heal me and to restore to me every bit of health and well-being I have lost through this sickness. Right now, You are faithfully upholding me, so I am not going to be afraid. And because You are holding on to me, I can let go and rest in You. It is Your faithfulness that will cause my healing to manifest. Thank You, Lord Jesus. Amen.

Beloved, just talking to Him like that *is* faith to Him. It is believing He is in your situation with you and that He is listening. And as you declare over the symptoms in your body that the One who has promised you healing is faithful, you are judging Him faithful, and you will see Him faithfully causing your healing to manifest.

CYST IN WOMB DISAPPEARS

Some years ago, the wife of one of my key leaders was diagnosed with a cyst in her womb. She went to different doctors to confirm the diagnosis, and the doctors all came to the conclusion that she had to undergo surgery to remove the cyst. She was told they might even have to remove her whole womb. Of course, this couple was very affected by the news. I met with them to pray with them and to partake of the holy Communion.

Honestly, I didn't feel any faith when I prayed for them. In fact, I felt quite helpless.

But I heard the Lord telling me to rest. I heard Him telling me not to even try to use faith and to simply rest in His faith. So I simply said, "Growth, I curse you to your roots in Jesus' name. Be plucked out by your roots and be thrown into the sea." At the same time, I also prayed the Lord would cause her youth to be renewed like the eagle's.

JUST TALKING TO GOD IS FAITH TO HIM.

A few days later, she was scheduled for a final scan before her surgery. And guess what? The doctors could not find the cyst! Her gynecologist said the whole growth had simply disappeared and that it was a miracle.

But the Lord didn't stop at removing the cyst in her womb. Remember how I prayed for her youth to be renewed? Her monthly period had actually stopped for some time, but soon after I prayed for her, it returned. The Lord had renewed her womb and her youth. Hallelujah!

I felt no faith when I prayed for her, so thank God her healing was not dependent on my faith. It is the faith of the faithful One, our Lord Jesus. That's why the holy Communion is so powerful. It puts your focus on Jesus and Him alone.

In the same way, even if you don't feel any faith when you are partaking of the holy Communion, don't stop. Don't focus on your faith or lack of it. Sometimes we confuse faith with emotions. Just put your trust in the One who never wavers. Don't give up!

10.

THE FIGHT TO REST

I don't know if you realize this, so I want to make it very clear: we are engaged in warfare.

In our modern world, many of us have access to doctors, hospitals, and various medications and treatments. And because we can just turn to Google for information about our symptoms and find out all about possible causes, treatment options, and contraindications for different medications, it is easy for us to forget there is an invisible realm. It is easy to forget there is a real enemy and that spiritual forces could be involved when we find ourselves under attack in our bodies.

There is an enemy who wants to destroy us, an enemy who wants to oppress us with sickness and stop us from reaping the harvest of health and divine life that is our inheritance as believers. I am not saying all diseases are caused by spirits, but let's not forget spirits exist. The gospel of Luke records how our Lord Jesus healed a woman who had been oppressed by a "spirit of infirmity" (Luke 13:10–17). For eighteen years she was bent over and could not raise herself up. Our Lord Jesus Himself said it was because *Satan* had bound her.

Thank God for doctors and nurses who have dedicated their lives to caring for the sick, preventing diseases, and alleviating the sufferings of their patients. They are a great blessing, and I fully believe God can work through them.

But there is a limit to what doctors can do when spiritual forces are involved, and we cannot use *natural* means to come against *supernatural* forces.

The apostle Paul wrote:

> For we do not wrestle against flesh and blood, but against principalities, against powers, against the rulers of the darkness of this age, against spiritual hosts of wickedness in the heavenly places. (Eph. 6:12)

Our fight is not against flesh and blood. Our warfare is a spiritual one.

SPIRITUAL WARFARE

For most people, spiritual warfare conjures up the idea of engaging in fierce battles with the devil. But some years ago, when I wrote a book titled *Spiritual Warfare*, do you know what I chose as the image for the cover of the book?

A picture of a man lying on a deck chair by the beach, with his arms folded languidly behind his head.

It's important to note that the whole passage about spiritual warfare in Ephesians 6 tells us over and over again to "stand" and mentions fighting only once, when it tells us that we do not "wrestle against flesh and blood" (Eph. 6:11–14).

Our fight is the fight to remain at rest and believe the work has already been finished. The only labor is the labor to enter the rest our Lord Jesus purchased for us at the cross. Our part is to *stand still* and see the salvation of the Lord. Let's stand in the victory Christ has already given us, instead of trying to defeat a foe that has *already* been defeated at the cross.

WHAT SPIRITUAL WARFARE LOOKS LIKE

I am not going to delve into teaching about spiritual warfare here, but to show you what it means to engage in spiritual warfare, let me share with you the precious journey taken by Anna.

Anna was part of the ministry team from Singapore that traveled to the United States for my Grace Revolution Tour. While she was in Dallas, Texas, she went through a horrifying ordeal. This is what she recounted:

> I started experiencing numbness in my legs that quickly progressed to my diaphragm. Unable to move, I was quickly brought to the emergency room where I underwent a five-hour emergency surgery for spinal cord compression caused by multiple lesions and tumorous growths along my entire spinal cord. I was later told I had stage-four cancer that had metastasized from the thoracic area to my neck and bones and was given a life expectancy of two to three years.

Can you imagine how terrifying it must have been for Anna? She shared with one of my pastors that before the day she was rushed to the emergency room, she had no idea cancer was spreading insidiously and silently throughout her entire spinal cord. Without warning, she found herself bedridden after surgery and facing a fight against stage-four cancer. She was hospitalized for more than a month. During this time and long after she was discharged, Anna fortified herself daily with the Word of God, garrisoning her heart against every fear and refusing to allow the enemy to shake her faith in the finished work of Christ. This is how she described her battle:

OUR FIGHT IS THE FIGHT TO REMAIN AT REST.

> All that I, a frightened sheep, could do was to just stay really close to the Great Shepherd. During my entire thirty-three days

of hospitalization (in Dallas and later back home in Singapore), Jesus became my impenetrable "safe house," protecting me from further assaults by the devil.

I requested for visitors to be kept to a minimum during my hospitalization, choosing to spend the time with the One whose very presence and words were now my very life and healing. Of course, I couldn't keep the doctors and nurses away, and sometimes, hearing the way they talked about my cancer caused the life and peace in me to leak—I felt that I had touched death.

But I remained in my "safe house," Jesus. And because I believe God's Word was life and health to all my flesh, I fed on God's Word during my waking hours, often drifting off to sleep, still plugged in to Pastor Prince's sermons playing on my iPad.

And every time I had to take my cancer medication, I would partake of the holy Communion at the same time. I did the same thing after undergoing each round of radiotherapy. And I believe that was the reason I didn't experience any of the side effects throughout my fifteen cycles of radiotherapy treatment. Except for hair loss that lasted only for a few months, my body (especially my blood cells, liver, and kidneys, which were areas of concern to my oncologist) has not shown any other side effects from my ongoing cancer medication even up till today, as I continue daily in the Word and in partaking of the holy Communion.

The cancer was real, and the tumors in her body were real. But Anna knew the true battle was a spiritual one. Of course, she was fearful. How could she not be? But she was a child of God, and she was not going to allow the enemy to intimidate her. Neither was she going to simply take his attacks lying down. She was going to fight back, armed with the sword of the Spirit (Eph. 6:17) and knowing that her God was backing her up all the way.

BE MORE CONSCIOUS OF YOUR GOD THAN OF YOUR ENEMY

Doesn't Anna remind you of David, the young shepherd boy who defeated the champion of the Philistine army? David did not run away when Goliath turned up. He got *angry* and demanded to know "who is this uncircumcised Philistine, that he should defy the armies of the living God?" (1 Sam. 17:26). The other soldiers were cowed by the size of their enemy. David was conscious only of how big his God was. Look at what he said when he came face-to-face with the giant:

> "You come to me with a sword, with a spear, and with a javelin. But *I come to you in the name of the* LORD *of hosts, the God of the armies of Israel*, whom you have defied." (1 Sam. 17:45)

DON'T TAKE THE ENEMY'S ATTACKS LYING DOWN. FIGHT BACK, ARMED WITH THE SWORD OF THE SPIRIT.

Beloved, if the enemy is trying to attack you with symptoms, I pray you catch David's spirit. Don't be afraid. Stand your ground and know that the enemy has already been defeated. His weapons might appear formidable to the world, but they are no match for your God. This battle is not yours to fight. The enemy may come against you with a sword, spear, and javelin, but when you come to him in the name of the Lord of hosts, that Goliath is no match for your God!

FORTIFY YOURSELF WITH THE WORD OF GOD

Coming back to Anna's journey, her doctors told her the very treatments that were supposed to help her fight the cancer cells could also destroy other vital parts of her body. Facts like these caused the life and peace in her to "leak." But instead of accepting these facts, she put on the full armor of God by standing resolutely on His finished work even when her situation appeared bleak.

In fact, I think she went beyond keeping herself in spiritual armor—she kept herself in the secret place of the Most High, allowing Him to be her refuge and fortress, taking Him as her deliverer (Ps. 91:1–3), and making Him her "impenetrable safe house" and her ark. He was her strong tower, her shield, and her Great Shepherd who protected her and carried her close to His heart.

> THE ENEMY MAY COME AGAINST YOU, BUT THAT GOLIATH IS NO MATCH FOR YOUR GOD.

She did not want to hear the groans of the other patients and the constant beeping of all the medical instruments in her ward or to keep looking at the death and sickness around her. So she immersed herself in the Word, listening to sermons, meditating on scriptures throughout the day, and partaking of the holy Communion daily.

She girded herself with the truth of the Word of God instead of accepting the medical facts. For instance, she shared with my team how the *fact* was her scans showed that her neck and spine had been attacked by the cancer. But she stood on the eternal *truth* of the living Word, which declares:

> The righteous person faces many troubles, but the LORD comes to the
> rescue each time. For *the LORD protects the bones of the righteous*; not
> one of them is broken! (Ps. 34:19–20 NLT)

> "It shall come to pass in that day that *his burden will be taken away
> from your shoulder, and his yoke from your neck*, and the yoke will be
> destroyed because of the anointing oil." (Isa. 10:27)

There were many other scriptures she stood on, and I just want to share some of them here. I pray they will strengthen you and help you to fight your battles:

He sent His word and healed them, and delivered them from their destructions. (Ps. 107:20)

And if Christ is in you, the body is dead because of sin, but *the Spirit is life* because of righteousness. But if the Spirit of Him who raised Jesus from the dead dwells in you, *He who raised Christ from the dead will also give life to your mortal bodies* through His Spirit who dwells in you. (Rom. 8:10–11)

"When they call on me, I will answer; I will be with them in trouble. I will rescue and honor them. I will reward them with a *long life* and give them my salvation." (Ps. 91:15–16 NLT)

As Anna kept feeding herself with scripture after scripture, I believe the Word of God literally became like medicine to her, and she grew stronger and stronger. After all, the book of Proverbs tells us that His words are "life to those who find them, and health to all their flesh" (Prov. 4:22).

THERE IS POWER IN GOD'S WORD

> PUT ON THE FULL ARMOR OF GOD BY STANDING RESOLUTELY ON HIS FINISHED WORK.

Whatever condition you are faced with, I want to encourage you to do what Anna did. Saturate yourself with the Word any way you can. Write out scriptures, listen to your audio Bible, listen to sermons about His finished work, and read books (like this one) that magnify all Jesus has done for you.

When you spend time in the Word of God, you can't help but reap its healing benefits. The Hebrew word for *health* is *marpe'*, which also means "a medicine" or "a cure."[1] Notice

Proverbs 4:22 says "health to *all* their flesh." Unlike many medications, the Word of God does not benefit one part of your body only to harm another part. It is health to your nose, to your knees, to your inner ear, to your intestines, to your skin—to *all* your flesh.

The Bible also declares that the Word of God is "living and powerful, and sharper than any two-edged sword, piercing even to the division of soul and spirit, and of joints and marrow" (Heb. 4:12). It is the opposite of death, and it is *powerful*.

No wonder our Lord Jesus, when explaining the parable of the sower, tells us that when the sower sows the Word, "Satan comes immediately and takes away the word that was sown in their hearts" (Mark 4:15).

Did you notice that the enemy comes *immediately*? Jesus was referring to the seeds that "fell by the wayside," but the principle I want you to see is that the enemy wants to steal the Word from our hearts because he does not want you to "believe and be saved" (Luke 8:5, 12). The devil knows that if you receive the Word and believe it, *you will be saved*. This is why he will do all he can to stop the Word of God from taking root in your heart. He knows that if it stays long enough, it will be your victory and his defeat!

> **THE WORD OF GOD IS HEALTH TO ALL YOUR FLESH.**

The word used for *saved* in the original Greek is the word *sozo*, which means "to save one from injury or peril; to save a suffering one from perishing, for example, one suffering from disease; to make well, heal, restore to health."[2]

The enemy knows how potent the Word of God is.

Do you?

No matter what channel you use to spend time in His Word, make sure you are well watered with the Word. As you keep yourself drenched and watered with the Word of God, I believe you will unconsciously and effortlessly get stronger and stronger, healthier and healthier.

SLOWLY BUT SURELY

AS YOU KEEP YOURSELF WATERED WITH THE WORD OF GOD, YOU WILL GET STRONGER AND HEALTHIER.

Anna's healing did not come overnight. She was bedridden for nine whole months and had to slowly learn to walk again. After going through radiotherapy treatment, she also had to go through hormonal chemotherapy. But she kept holding on to the Lord's promises, and she kept partaking of the Communion, remembering all He had done for her.

The friends who were on this journey with her shared how they saw her healing take place slowly but surely.

The first time they visited her in the hospital, she could not even sit up. The next time they visited her, she was able to push herself up using the hospital bedrails.

When they first visited her at her home after she was discharged, she could not walk to the door. Her family member had to open the door for them. Sometime later, when they visited her again, she could make her way to the front door with the help of a walking frame. That was soon replaced with a walking stick.

Today Anna walks around freely without any aids. It took two years, but she is now back at work in my ministry office. And every opportunity she gets to pray for her colleagues who are unwell, she grabs. Indeed, the Lord has strengthened her and lengthened her days.

As for the cancer, her tumor marker was still above 150 after she completed her radiotherapy treatment. But it has since fallen way below the acceptable reading of <35.0. The Lord used medical technology in her healing process, but as she continues "daily in the Word and in partaking of the holy Communion," He has kept her protected from the negative side effects of the radiation and medication that many others have experienced.

Hallelujah! All glory to Jesus!

It is vital for believers to understand that faith in the Lord's healing power doesn't mean you don't seek medical advice or discontinue your medical treatment. Faith and medicine don't have to be mutually exclusive. In fact, I believe God uses doctors, and I have taught my church to pray that the Lord will anoint the hands of their surgeons if they have to undergo surgery and that the Lord will give their doctors the wisdom to give accurate diagnoses and decide on the best treatments.

Faith isn't about throwing away your medication, stopping your prescribed treatments, or avoiding surgical procedures. Praise the Lord for all the advancements made in medical science. They have done so much to improve the quality of our lives and to help people live longer. Doctors and medical professionals are fighting the same battles against sickness and disease that we are, and I have nothing but respect and honor for them.

FAITH AND MEDICINE DON'T HAVE TO BE MUTUALLY EXCLUSIVE.

In Anna's case, her doctors were rightfully fulfilling their responsibilities by informing her of the possible side effects of the treatment they were about to put her through. But while she went ahead with the treatments, her confidence for her total healing and complete restoration was entirely in her Savior and the Shepherd of her soul, our Lord Jesus Christ. She put her trust wholly in the Lord and in the holy Communion, believing she would not experience negative side effects. And praise the Lord, she experienced minimal side effects. If you are struggling with this conflict of faith versus medicine, I pray Anna's living testimony will be a great source of encouragement to you and help you experience His supernatural peace.

FAITH WORKS IN PARTNERSHIP WITH PATIENCE

I also want you to see that Anna's healing took place over a period of time. Sometimes, when the manifestation of our healing takes longer than what we hope for, the enemy can start to play mind games with us.

Maybe you have been partaking of the holy Communion for some time but have yet to see the results you want, and you are starting to entertain thoughts that maybe the Communion is just a superstitious practice, an empty ritual that does not do anything for you.

May I tell you there is spiritual warfare going on to get you to give up on the very channel God has ordained to bring supernatural life and health into your body?

As I mentioned in the previous chapter, miracles of instantaneous healing *can* take place. But our Lord Jesus also tells us what to expect when we are trusting Him for a breakthrough that does not manifest instantly. Notice what He says about how the seeds of the Word of God bear fruit when they fall on good ground:

> "But these are the ones sown on good ground, those who hear the word, accept it, and bear fruit: *some thirtyfold, some sixty, and some a hundred.*" (Mark 4:20)

Luke's gospel records:

> "But as for that seed in the good soil, these are the ones who have heard the word with a good and noble heart, and *hold on to it tightly, and bear fruit with patience.*" (Luke 8:15 AMP)

Do you notice the seeds that fall on good ground "bear fruit with patience"? "Patience" refers to perseverance and endurance.

Do you know why patience is involved?

Because *it takes time for seeds to bear fruit.* It does not happen overnight. Just as the farmer waits patiently for the precious fruit of the earth, you also need to be patient (James 5:7). Your harvest will come incrementally—first thirtyfold, then sixtyfold, then a hundredfold.

When you begin to partake of the Communion, you might see some improvements, but the pain is mostly still there. That's a thirtyfold harvest.

Don't give up!

Keep on partaking of the holy Communion by faith until you get your sixtyfold harvest. That's when you know there has been major improvement—you can even feel it—but maybe some symptoms are still there, lingering on.

That's the time to keep persevering, and to keep trusting, and to keep putting your eyes on His finished work until you see your hundredfold harvest of blessings, and you experience full healing for your condition.

> YOUR HARVEST WILL COME INCREMENTALLY— FIRST THIRTYFOLD, THEN SIXTYFOLD, THEN A HUNDREDFOLD.

YOUR HUNDREDFOLD HARVEST IS COMING

When you are faced with pain in your body, or you are so tired of hearing one negative report after another, I know the last thing you want to do is to endure another moment of the symptoms. But even if you don't see your healing immediately, please don't allow the enemy to sell you the lie that you should just give up because your healing is never going to happen.

Keep on watering the seed of the Word of God and wait patiently until it takes root. In due season, you will reap your harvest (Gal. 6:9).

The Bible tells us how Abraham obtained the promise after he had "patiently endured" (Heb. 6:15). Even though God had sworn to bless him and make him a great nation (Gen. 12:2), there was a fight of faith involved. The blessing did not manifest the next day. It did not manifest even in the next year. In fact, it took about twenty-five years before Abraham and Sarah had Isaac (Gen. 21:5). I am not saying you have to wait twenty-five years. The principle I want you to see here is that it might take some time, but you *will* inherit your promise.

Your healing might not be immediate, but believe that it is on its way. If you have been waiting for a while now for your healing and you are feeling discouraged, let God's promise strengthen you:

> "For as the rain comes down, and the snow from heaven,
> And do not return there,
> But water the earth,
> And make it bring forth and bud,
> That it may give seed to the sower
> And bread to the eater,
> So shall My word be that goes forth from My mouth;
> It shall not return to Me void,
> But it shall accomplish what I please,
> And it shall prosper in the thing for which I sent it."
> (Isa. 55:10–11)

God's Word will not return to Him void. Maybe you have partaken of the Communion, and you have prayed, but nothing seems to be happening. Maybe it has even come to the point you feel like you are just going through the motions because discouragement has set in. What do you do?

KEEP ON WATERING THE SEED OF GOD'S WORD. IN DUE SEASON, YOU WILL REAP YOUR HARVEST.

Keep on watering the seed of the Word of God with the rain of His Word!

When a seed is sown, you don't see anything immediately, but you know it *will* begin to sprout leaves and grow. You don't have to keep digging up the soil to check if the seed is growing. In the same way, when the seed of the Word of God is sown, your part is to have faith in the power of His Word and to be patient, as you believe that His words shall not return to Him void. And just as the earth yields crops incrementally, "first the blade, then the head, after that the full grain in the head" (Mark 4:28), I declare that you shall reap the full harvest of your healing!

THE GROUND IS READY FOR YOUR HEALING

I am going to share with you a revelation the Lord gave me some years ago. I have never heard anyone else teach this, and I know it is going to bless you.

HAVE FAITH IN THE POWER OF HIS WORD AND BE PATIENT. HIS WORDS SHALL NOT RETURN TO HIM VOID.

While our Lord Jesus uses the analogy of the sower and the seed to teach us about the Word of God, we also find graphic agricultural imagery being used to help us understand the violent suffering He endured for our healing. Read this verse with me:

"The plowers plowed on my back; they made their furrows long."
(Ps. 129:3)

Psalm 129 is a messianic psalm, and this is a picture of the scourging our Lord Jesus went through. I was reading this verse one day, and I felt the Lord saying to me, "Don't rush through reading this. Meditate on why I used words that are associated with farming."

Why didn't the Lord say, "They beat My back," or even, "They scourged My back"? Why didn't He use words like *hit* or *smite*?

Instead, He said, "The plowers plowed on my back; they made their furrows long."

Plowers drag a sharp plow that digs into the soil to break up the soil and make deep furrows in preparation for seeds to be sown. Let me show you a picture of what furrows look like:

*Furrows made in the ground by a plow allow for the planting of seeds and irrigation.
In Psalm 129, the furrows speak of the scourging Jesus received for our healing.*

I believe that was what happened to our Lord Jesus' back. When He was scourged by the Roman soldiers, it was as if His whole back had been plowed.

Victims of Roman flagellation were scourged using a flagellum or cat-o-nine-tails, a whip made up of several long leather thongs embedded with shards of broken bone, metal, and hooks. With each stroke, the thongs would wrap around the victim's body, and the shards would lodge in his flesh. When it was jerked away, the skin of the victim would be ripped off, and his flesh would be gouged out and left in shreds.[3]

Every one of these stripes tore our Lord's flesh, making deep, long furrows across His back. By the time His tormentors were done, I believe there wasn't a single sliver of skin left on His back. Psalm 22, a messianic psalm, tells us that even His bones were exposed and stared back at Him (Ps. 22:17).

And this is what the Lord showed me: it was not by coincidence the language of sowing was used to describe the horrific scourging our Lord Jesus went through.

Furrows are made so that seeds can be sown.

When you feel like you have no faith to believe in healing, the Word of God says you just need faith as small as a mustard seed (Luke 17:6).

So it is not about how strong your faith is—just sow your little seeds of faith into the good ground of our Lord. The more you see what He has done for you, and how He allowed His back to be plowed for you, the more your faith will grow and the more you will experience a harvest of healing.

When His back was lashed into furrows, He was allowing the seed for your healing from high blood pressure to be sown. He was allowing the seed for the healing of that tumor to be sown. He was allowing the seed for healing of your child's asthma and eczema to be sown. Whatever condition you or your loved one might be suffering from, Jesus' suffering and sacrifice—the plowing and long furrows made on His back—speak of how the price for your healing has been paid in full. Now reach out by faith and receive your healing.

You are so loved.

So, so loved.

Whenever you partake of the Communion, remember Him. Our Lord Jesus suffered every sickness on your behalf so that you would not have to go through the pain. He bore your sicknesses and diseases in His own body. He carried your physical pains and your mental sorrows. He was wounded for your sins and transgressions. He was crushed for your iniquities. The punishment with a view to your health and well-being fell upon Him.

THE PRICE FOR YOUR HEALING HAS BEEN PAID IN FULL.

And by His stripes *you are healed* (Isa. 53:4–5).

You might still be trusting God for the symptoms to leave your body, but I already know the outcome of this matter. It is not over until His victory is gloriously manifested. May you be conscious of the Lord Himself building you up and strengthening you with His Word, countering every attack with His truth, and guarding your heart against every lie of the enemy. And even as you wait for your hundredfold harvest, may you experience His love for you like never before!

11.

GOD OF YOUR VALLEYS

I pray your eyes have been opened to the amazing truths about the holy Communion and that you are excited about the revelations you have received. If you are facing a medical challenge, I pray the Lord has used this book to impart hope, life, and strength to you. Maybe you have even gotten hold of Communion elements and have started to partake of them. If so, praise the Lord! Keep persevering till you receive your breakthrough.

But maybe you are thinking, *I have read so many testimonies, and it feels like everyone else has received their breakthroughs and they are experiencing their mountaintops. But where is God in my situation? Am I going to stay in this valley forever?*

BECAUSE HE IS WITH YOU EVEN IN YOUR VALLEY, HAVE CONFIDENCE THAT YOU WILL COME THROUGH IT.

Beloved, I want you to know He never leaves you nor forsakes you (Heb. 13:5). He is near to those who are brokenhearted (Ps. 34:18), and right now He is drawn to you in your situation as you cry out to Him. He is both the God of the mountaintops and the God of the valleys (1 Kings 20:28). He is with you even in the valley, and because of that, you can have the confidence that you *will* get through it (Ps. 23:4).

I really believe knowing the truths about the holy Communion can mean the difference between life and death for you and your loved ones. This is not something I say lightly. In fact, I experienced the healing power of the holy Communion for myself as I was writing this book.

ACCELERATED RECOVERY THROUGH COMMUNION

My son, Justin, had just entered first grade in a new school and had been there for only about a month. During his recess one day, he somehow fell from a structure in the schoolyard and hurt his head. His teachers called us to let us know Justin was in the general office crying because he had fallen at the playground. My wife, Wendy, headed down to the school as she happened to be nearby. It is not unusual for kids to fall down while playing, so Wendy wasn't too concerned.

We believe it was the Lord who prompted Wendy to ask Justin to show her exactly where he had fallen. When Justin showed Wendy the height he had fallen from, her heart grew cold and she knew she had to take him to the hospital for a thorough checkup.

At the hospital, the doctors put him through a CT scan and discovered he had fractured his skull.

After he started throwing up, they decided to conduct a more detailed scan. This time, they found another fracture in his skull they had not detected earlier. They also discovered some bleeding in his skull where the fracture happened, as well as blood in his middle ear.

It was heart-wrenching for me to watch my little six-year-old boy crying and clutching his head, twisting and turning in a vain attempt to stop the intense pain. My normally lively Justin suddenly became weak and lethargic, and it didn't help that he was throwing up and could not eat. It was also not easy for me to look at the scans and listen to his doctor talk about the possible effect of the injury on Justin's brain. Fear crept into my heart, and it was truly a fight to remain at rest.

Apart from giving him painkillers and monitoring him, the doctors couldn't do much for Justin. But Wendy and I knew God could, and we decided to partake of the Communion with Justin. During the entire period of his hospitalization, we partook of the Communion with him at least three or four times each day. The amazing thing was, we could literally see him getting better and better each time we partook. Every time we had the Communion with Justin, his headaches got less painful, to the point when he told us he would rather just partake of the Communion than take the painkillers the doctors had given him.

We know that it was the Lord who accelerated Justin's healing and helped him to get well in record time. The doctors expected Justin to take at least six weeks to get better, but he improved so quickly that in less than three weeks, they gave him the all clear to return to school.

All glory to Jesus!

THE LORD GOES BEFORE YOU AND IS WITH YOU IN YOUR TRIAL

During what Justin went through, I experienced for myself something I want you to be aware of if you are facing a trial right now: God is not far away. He is *with* you. He loves you, and He is your very present help.

> GOD IS NOT FAR AWAY. HE IS WITH YOU. HE LOVES YOU, AND HE IS YOUR VERY PRESENT HELP.

Throughout Justin's time in the hospital, Wendy and I were very conscious of the Lord's hand of protection upon our child. His injuries could have been so much worse. The fractures narrowly missed the main blood vessels in his head, which would have led to a hemorrhage and could have damaged his brain. There also was a bone fragment that somehow got pushed away from his brain instead of being lodged in it.

As his parents, there is no way we can keep him in a cocoon and protect him twenty-four hours a day, but we saw how the Lord Himself protected Justin and saved him from sustaining injuries that could have been much more devastating.

In the same way, I want you to know the Lord watches over you and your loved ones. Because He neither slumbers nor sleeps (Ps. 121:4–5 NIV), you can rest in the assurance that even while you sleep, He works the night shift. He will deliver you and keep you from falling (Ps. 56:13). All the devices of the enemy will be confounded, and even if a weapon has been formed against you, it shall not prosper!

THE LORD WATCHES OVER YOU. EVEN WHILE YOU SLEEP, HE WORKS THE NIGHT SHIFT.

You read Anna's story in the last chapter. But there is actually more. Although Anna had gone through a harrowing experience, it was clear the Lord was with her through it all. She wrote:

> Looking back, had I not gone on this work trip, I would not have been in Dallas. Had I not been in Dallas, I would not have been operated on by a Christian surgeon who personally told me that it is not him but Jesus who heals. And had I not been operated on at that time, my numbing paralysis would soon have become too far advanced and the outcome could have been so different. I could have become an invalid from my neck down, or the cancer could have killed me. I shudder even to think about it!
>
> And had I not paid US$17 to top up the travel insurance provided for this work trip, I would not have had my huge hospital bill, which came up to over US$200,000, borne entirely by the travel insurance company! All this can only be the Lord's doing, and it is marvelous in my eyes (Ps. 118:23). To God be all the glory and praise! Praise Jesus!

Isn't it amazing to see how the Lord had divinely orchestrated for Anna to be in Dallas, where she "happened" to be sent to a particular hospital, where according to her nurse, her surgeon "happened" to be among the top ten spinal surgeons in America, one whom even professional athletes would seek out?

She shared with my team that even if she had found out about her cancer earlier, there was no way she could have afforded the medical fees to go through the surgery even in Singapore, let alone performed by a top surgeon in America. The Lord truly went before her and caused *all* things to work together for her good (Rom. 8:28).

My friend, whatever you might be going through, put your trust in the Lord. You might feel helpless against that disease or that ballooning medical bill, but don't lose hope. Just as He was working behind the scenes to position Anna at the right place at the right time and to ensure that her entire surgery and hospitalization cost was paid for, trust that He is working behind the scenes for you.

TRUST THAT HE IS WORKING BEHIND THE SCENES FOR YOU.

Trust that His grace is sufficient for you, for His *strength* is made perfect in your weakness (2 Cor. 12:9). The Greek root word used for *strength* is the word *dunamis*, which refers to the miracle-working power of God.[1] You don't have to try to be strong in and of yourself. His miracle-working power is made perfect in your time of weakness. You will get through this trial. Not only that, I am believing with you that you will emerge even stronger than before.

JESUS COMES TO YOU IN YOUR VALLEY

I don't know what valley you are in right now, but I want to share a very powerful picture in the Bible that I pray will encourage you.

Every time something is mentioned in the Bible for the first time, it is always significant. Do you know where you find the Communion—the bread and the wine—mentioned together for the first time? Let me show you:

> Then Melchizedek king of Salem brought out *bread and wine*; he was the priest of God Most High. And he blessed him and said: "Blessed be Abram of God Most High, Possessor of heaven and earth; and blessed be God Most High, who has delivered your enemies into your hand." (Gen. 14:18–20)

Who is Melchizedek? The Bible tells us that our Lord Jesus is "a priest forever according to the order of Melchizedek" (Heb. 7:17). Many scholars believe he is a pre-incarnate appearance of Christ. But it is clear that Melchizedek is a type of Christ.

Melchizedek was the king of Salem, which means "peace." But Salem means much more than peace. It also means "complete, safe, perfect, whole, and full."[2]

Melchizedek met Abram in the Valley of Shaveh, or the King's Valley (Gen. 14:17). I did a study of the location of the King's Valley and realized it is actually in the Kidron Valley. *Kidron* in Hebrew is from the word *qadar*, which means "darkness."[3]

Melchizedek wasn't the only person present with Abram. Bera, the king of Sodom, went out to meet Abram before Melchizedek arrived (Gen. 14:2, 17). Bera's name in Hebrew means "son of evil."[4]

I gave you all that background because I want you to see this: *when you are in a place of darkness, your Lord Jesus comes to you, bearing bread and wine.*

THE COMMUNION IS NOT SOMETHING YOU DO; IT'S SOMETHING YOU RECEIVE.

You might be asking, "Won't the Communion become something legalistic that I *have* to do?" Not if you see yourself receiving the bread and the wine from the Lord Jesus Himself. The Communion is not something that you do; you *receive* the Communion just as Abram did.

Whatever valley you might be in right now, whatever evil you might be faced with, you are not alone.

May your eyes be opened to see that the King of peace is with you. The King of completeness, of safety, and of wholeness is with you, and He comes bearing bread and wine for you. He comes to refresh you and to impart to you His shalom.

In your time of darkness, don't forget that the Lord has given you the Communion as a tangible, practical way of remembering all He has done for you.

Don't think that you have to handle the situation all by yourself. The Lord is with you, and He wants you to bring Him every fear and every worry. Talk to Him. Whenever I am afraid I like to sing the words from the psalms of David to strengthen myself in the Lord. May you be filled with His strength as you meditate on and worship Him with these words from the psalmist:

> You are my hiding place;
> You shall preserve me from trouble;
> You shall surround me with songs of deliverance.
> Whenever I am afraid,
> I will trust in You. (Ps. 32:7; 56:3)

WE ALL GO THROUGH VALLEYS

Abram was in a valley immediately after he had secured a great victory. You might be fresh from a victory—maybe you exceeded all your sales targets or you just experienced a breakthrough—but very quickly you can find yourself in a valley. This is why we cannot put our confidence in temporal things. Everyone, no matter what successes they have enjoyed, is susceptible to times of darkness in their lives.

In the same way, just because I am a pastor and I teach on the Communion, it does not mean that I am not confronted with challenges. I know the same is true for other pastors as well, so if you can, please keep your pastors and leaders in prayer—you don't know what they might be going through.

Wendy and I went through a difficult period in our lives. A few years after we had our daughter, Jessica, Wendy became pregnant with our second child, and we were looking forward to meeting our baby. Then, nine weeks into her pregnancy, the doctor told us the baby had no heartbeat. I have never seen Wendy cry the way she cried, and I pray I never will again. Our hearts were broken. All we could do was weep.

WE DON'T HAVE ALL THE ANSWERS, BUT WE KNOW GOD IS GOOD

Maybe you are going through a difficult valley yourself. Maybe you are disappointed with God because you have lost a loved one or because you have been battling that medical condition year after year.

I want to encourage you not to ask, "Why?" Asking why will only lead you on a downward spiral into depression. Don't ask, "Why did this happen to me?" Don't ask, "Why is my child not healed even though I have trusted You for years?" or "Why is my loved one going through one tragedy after another?"

The fact is, in this fallen world, we don't have all the answers. One day, we will receive our new bodies, where the corruptible will put on incorruption, and the mortal will put on immortality (1 Cor. 15:53). But until then, I recognize that sometimes bad things happen and I don't know *why*.

But what I *do know* is this: God is a good God. He loves us, and He is *never* behind any pain we go through. Our faith in Him is not based on our experiences; it is based on the unchanging, eternal Word of God, which cannot lie.

GOD'S RESTORATION IS ALWAYS GREATER

> **GOD LOVES YOU AND IS NEVER BEHIND ANY PAIN THAT YOU GO THROUGH.**

When Wendy and I first lost our baby, our pain was too raw, and honestly, it was hard for us to feel faith in our emotions. But like I said, faith is not about emotions. Even though we were crushed, we continued to trust Him.

By faith, we told the Lord, "We don't understand all that happened, but we know You are a good God. We know You are not behind this, and we put our trust in You. We won't give up on Your promises. You love us, and we know You have a child in store for us, and that child will be a champion." We started to partake of the Communion together as we believed God for a baby, and I even decided to ask the Lord for a baby boy.

Today I want you to know that Wendy and I may have lost our baby, but we have also received our restoration. It took some time, but Justin David Prince came along, and what a restoration he is!

Whatever you may have lost, we are believing with you for your restoration.

YOUR LOVED ONES IN HEAVEN ARE PERFECTLY HEALTHY AND WHOLE

If you have lost a child as we have, I want you to know that your child is growing up in heaven. When David's child died, he said, "I will go to him one day, but he cannot return to me" (2 Sam. 12:23 NLT). That's why as far as Wendy and I are concerned, we have three children. Two are here on earth and one is in heaven.

And if you have loved ones who have passed on, don't be discouraged. If they are believers, you will see them again. They have just relocated to a place where there is no sickness, no pain, no adversity, and they are more alive than any of us.

GOD CAN RESTORE EVEN THE STOLEN YEARS

Even when things didn't go the way you wanted them to, don't remain in your disappointment. The devil wants you to get angry with God and to give up on His promises. But keep believing that God is *for* you and not against you. Even if the enemy has destroyed something in your life, and even if years have been lost as you waited for the manifestation of your healing, or the days of your youth have been stolen from you, keep believing that God can restore to you what you have lost (Joel 2:25; Job 33:25).

My friend, "let us hold fast the confession of our hope without wavering, for He who promised is faithful" (Heb. 10:23). Keep on looking *to* the Lord for your breakthrough. And if you find that you are too tired to believe anymore, I pray that this promise will carry you through:

> **GOD IS FOR YOU AND NOT AGAINST YOU.**

But those who wait on the LORD shall renew their strength; they shall mount up with wings like eagles, they shall run and not be weary, they shall walk and not faint. (Isa. 40:31)

FIND FRIENDS WHO CAN CARRY YOU WHEN YOUR FAITH IS WEAK

Sometimes it is difficult for us to have faith when we are on our own. When you have no strength and no faith, you need others to pull you through. I want to share with you a precious testimony from Audrey, a leader in my church who experienced that for herself. I have shared just part of her testimony here:

> In the twenty-ninth week of my pregnancy, my water bag broke because of an infection, and I was admitted to the hospital for bed rest.
>
> That week, if a day passed without any sign of labor, it was a

miracle. Friends who knew about our situation prayed with us, encouraged us, and believed with us for the birth of a healthy baby. My husband and I also partook of the holy Communion as frequently as we were able to.

In the thirtieth week, I started to have contractions and bleeding, and baby Jenna was born, weighing 1.5 kg (3.3 lb). We thank God that she had no major complications. She was able to breathe on her own without oxygen support. All her organs were intact and functioning properly despite her premature birth.

She stayed in the neonatal ICU for seven days, and in the special care unit until she was thirty-six weeks old. During this period, we saw how she gradually progressed from a tiny baby supported by tubes and needles, to tube feeding and finally to normal feeding.

But truth be told, the daily commute to the hospital was tiring. I was thankful for kingdom friends who kept us in prayer. Many of them partook of the holy Communion on their own as they prayed for us. Our firstborn daughter also reminded us to receive the Communion for her little sister.

Praise the Lord, despite being born about two months premature, baby Jenna did not face major health complications, and after forty days in the hospital, she was finally allowed to go home.

Unfortunately, Audrey's joy at being able to bring her baby home was short-lived. She shared that after they brought baby Jenna home, they noticed she was very drowsy and did not even cry for milk. They decided to take her back to the hospital, where a few days later she was placed in the ICU as her heart rate suddenly became critically low due to a virus that had affected her heart.

Audrey wrote:

I was devastated. *How much more did her little 2 kg body have to go through?* I cried to the Lord. I was out of prayer and out of faith, but my husband kept encouraging me to look to Jesus, to how He had already paid the price for Jenna's healing. Healing is bread for the children of God, he reminded me. Our leaders and close friends in church also never stopped praying for Jenna.

Thank God for her husband, church friends, and leaders who rallied around her, prayed with her, and partook of the holy Communion on behalf of baby Jenna when Audrey was "out of prayer and out of faith." Every one of those friends had a part to play in the victory they experienced, and the Lord used them to surround Audrey and her husband in an environment of faith even when they kept meeting with setbacks. Likewise, I pray that you will also have a community of kingdom friends who can bring you to Jesus when you have no strength to carry on.

During that period, Audrey shared that I preached a fresh message about the Communion in church, and after she heard it, she and her husband determined that they were not going to give up partaking of the holy Communion and claiming restoration for Jenna.

KINGDOM FRIENDS CAN BRING YOU TO JESUS WHEN YOU HAVE NO STRENGTH TO CARRY ON.

In the days that followed Jenna's second hospital stay, more challenges followed: from critically low, her heart rate became too high. But Audrey and her husband persevered and kept partaking of the Communion for baby Jenna until finally she was out of danger. It was an arduous journey for them, but their baby went home healthy and strong. Hallelujah! Audrey shared:

As I think of how Jesus healed the paralytic based on the faith of the four friends who lowered him through the roof, I thank God we also had these "four friends." Our friends continually prayed for Jenna, encouraged us to press in to claim God's healing, and to partake of the holy Communion.

And as I think of the two months of evil days we spent in the hospital, I am sure God will restore to us many, many good days ahead. He will restore to us everything that was stolen from us during those dark days!

Amen and amen. Praise the Lord!

If you have been dealing with a long, drawn-out medical condition or you are exhausted from caring for a loved one who has been sick for a long time, depression can creep in as the burden gets too heavy for you. My friend, bring your cares, bring that burden to Him. He cares about you with deepest affection and watches over you so very carefully (1 Peter 5:7 AMP). At the same time, I want you to know God never meant for you to function in a vacuum. His heart is for you to be planted in a local church. The Bible encourages us not to forsake "the assembling of ourselves together" but to exhort and encourage one another, especially as the day of His return draws near (Heb. 10:25).

> HE CARES ABOUT YOU WITH DEEPEST AFFECTION AND WATCHES OVER YOU SO VERY CAREFULLY.

If you are not planted in a local church, may I encourage you to consider finding one? One of the tactics of the enemy is to try to take you away from the body of Christ and isolate you. That's what he did to the Gadarene demoniac, who withdrew from society to live among the tombs (Mark 5:1–5). Don't let him do that to you.

Come home to the church. The church is not perfect by any means. But we have a perfect Savior who has done a perfect work on the cross, and there is safety, healing, and provision in the house of God.

12.

PURSUE THE HEALER

I love the fact that of all the words God could have chosen to call this beautiful meal, He chose the word *Communion*. It speaks of the relationship God wants to have with us, the closeness and intimacy He desires to have with us. I know it can be easy to lose sight of that and even see the Communion as a means to an end, especially when you are battling symptoms in your body. But as you continue to come to the Lord's Table, don't just go after the healing and miss the One who prepared the table for you. Pursue the healer and not just the healing. Pursue the blesser and not just the blessing. When you have Him, you have everything.

I want to encourage you with one of my favorite stories in the New Testament. As we come to the end of this book, I pray that you are not walking away with mere *information* about what the holy Communion is, but you have experienced what the two disciples did on the road to Emmaus when "*Jesus Himself drew near and went with them*" (Luke 24:15).

> PURSUE THE HEALER AND NOT JUST THE HEALING. WHEN YOU HAVE HIM, YOU HAVE EVERYTHING.

That journey to Emmaus took place the very day our Lord Jesus rose bodily from the grave. What was so important to the Lord that He would do it on the day of His resurrection?

The resurrected Christ did this:

And beginning at Moses and all the Prophets, *He expounded to them in all the Scriptures the things concerning Himself.* (Luke 24:27)

Later the two disciples said to each other, *"Did not our heart burn within us* while He talked with us on the road, and while He opened the Scriptures to us?"* (Luke 24:32).

As a pastor, that is what I endeavor to do every Sunday, and that is what I pray I have accomplished through the pages of this book. I pray that by the grace of God, I have been able to expound to you in the Scriptures, not a list of rules and regulations, not knowledge that puffs up the intellect, but things concerning *Himself.*

I pray that your heart burned within you as you saw Jesus in the Scriptures and you have experienced His deep, personal love for you as never before. I pray that you have felt Jesus *Himself* drawing near to you, lavishing His love on you and imparting to you all that you need. And beyond what He can do for you or your loved one, beyond healing for that condition that you might have been battling with, I pray that you have had an encounter with the Lord Jesus *Himself.*

THE CURSE HAS BEEN REVERSED

There were many important people our Lord could have appeared to, but before He appeared to even Peter, James, and John, He chose to appear to these two disciples on the road to Emmaus. Why?

I believe the Lord was about to go on a journey of restoration. I am so excited about this I can hardly contain myself. Don't miss this, because I believe what you are about to read will blow your mind and heal your body as well. I want you to watch the restoration unfolding. Are you with me?

Look with me at what happened in the garden of Eden where the Lord walked with *two*—Adam and Eve (Gen. 3:8):

> So when the woman saw that the tree was good for food, that it was pleasant to the eyes, and a tree desirable to make one wise, *she took of its fruit and ate. She also gave to her husband with her, and he ate. Then the eyes of both of them were opened, and they knew that they were naked.* (Gen. 3:6–7)

They ate from the Tree of Knowledge of Good and Evil. And their eyes were opened—to their nakedness.

Through that act of eating from a tree, sin and death entered the world (Rom. 5:12). Man was never meant to have disease, sickness, or pain. Man was never meant to grow old and die. God hates death. This is why He called death an enemy (1 Cor. 15:26). Our Lord Jesus even wept at Lazarus's death (John 11:35).

But look at how God reversed everything.

KNOW HIM THROUGH THE COMMUNION

Most people assume the two disciples whom Jesus walked with on the road to Emmaus were men, even though only one man—Cleopas—was named. I have many reasons to believe the other disciple was a woman, and the two were likely husband and wife. For instance, they said to each other, "Did not *our heart* burn within us while He talked with us on the road, and while He opened the Scriptures to us?" (Luke 24:32). Shouldn't it have been "our hearts" and not "our heart" since

GOD HATES DEATH. THIS IS WHY HE CALLS DEATH AN ENEMY.

there were two of them? I submit to you that they were married and saw themselves as one (Gen. 2:24).

In any case, look at what happened with the two disciples at the end of the journey to Emmaus. Sin and death came in through an act of eating, and we are about to see Jesus restore everything that was lost in the garden of Eden, through another act of eating:

> Now it came to pass, as He sat at the table with them, that *He took bread, blessed and broke it, and gave it to them.* Then their eyes were opened and they knew Him. (Luke 24:30–31)

While the two disciples were walking to Emmaus with Jesus, their eyes had been restrained and the Lord prevented them from recognizing Him (Luke 24:16). But the moment they took the bread from Jesus, the Bible tells us that "their eyes were opened." But this time, unlike Adam and Eve, their eyes were not opened to their nakedness. Their eyes were opened so that "they knew Him."

The word *knew* here is the Greek word *epiginosko*, which means "full or intimate knowledge or revelation."[1] In other words, when they took the bread and ate it, their eyes were opened to perceive who it really was in their midst—the Messiah they had followed, who had brought healing, restoration, and life to so many, and who had defeated death! Later, the two disciples spoke about the things that had happened on the road, particularly "how He was known to them in the breaking of bread" (Luke 24:33–35).

What is this bread that could cause the two disciples to *know* Jesus?

PARTAKE OF THE TREE OF LIFE

Luke 24:30 records that "He took bread, blessed and broke it, and gave it to them."

Doesn't this remind you of another time when Jesus took bread, blessed and broke it, and gave it to the disciples, saying, "Take, eat; this is My body" (Matt. 26:26; Mark 14:22)?

The resurrected Christ had the holy *Communion* with the two disciples! What an honor the Lord Jesus has put on the breaking of bread, on this wonderful sacrament He has given to the church.

Pastors and leaders, I believe the Lord was showing us what must happen in our churches every Sunday. First, He showed us how we must teach from "all the Scriptures," including Moses and all the Prophets, the things concerning *Himself* (Luke 24:27). I believe the two disciples' eyes were *restrained* from recognizing Him physically (Luke 24:16), because to the Lord it was more important for them to see Him in the Scriptures than to see Him in person.

Second, the Lord put the holy Communion on a divine pedestal and made it central. This is why in my church, we receive the Communion every single week. That's what the early church did as well. The book of Acts tells us that the disciples "came together to break bread" on "the first day of the week" (Acts 20:7). Shouldn't we emphasize what our Lord Jesus put emphasis on?

> **THE LORD PUT THE HOLY COMMUNION ON A DIVINE PEDESTAL AND MADE IT CENTRAL. SHOULDN'T WE EMPHASIZE WHAT HE PUT EMPHASIS ON?**

When God made Adam and Eve, He made them complete except for one thing: their spiritual eyes were not opened. God wanted their spiritual eyes to be opened by the Tree of Life, but instead they partook of the Tree of Knowledge of Good and Evil, and their eyes were opened to see their nakedness. Their eyes were opened to see their failures and shortcomings, their lack and their inadequacies, their sin and their shame.

But our Lord Jesus was restoring all that was lost in that garden. I believe when He broke bread for the two disciples, He was letting them eat from the Tree of Life, the tree that God had wanted man to eat from. Our

Lord Jesus *is* the Tree of Life, and when we partake of His broken body, we are eating from the Tree of Life. That is why the moment the two disciples took the bread, *their eyes were opened,* and they knew the Lord Jesus. The apostle Paul also prayed that our eyes may be opened, that we may see Jesus, that we may truly have a revelation of His love (Eph. 1:17–18; 3:18–19). I had been searching the Scriptures for years to find out more about the Tree of Life and was so excited when the Lord showed me this.

After the two disciples partook of the Tree of Life, I believe something happened to their bodies: they were infused and energized with the resurrection life of Christ. This was why they could rise up that very hour to walk back to Jerusalem (Luke 24:33), covering fourteen miles in one day (Luke 24:13). Today we can rejoice because that same resurrection life flows into our bodies each time we partake of the Lord's Supper.

> **HIS RESURRECTION LIFE FLOWS INTO OUR BODIES EACH TIME WE PARTAKE OF THE LORD'S SUPPER.**

Adam and Eve ate their way to the curse, and with it, sickness, stress, diseases, pain, and death. You and I get to partake of the Tree of Life whenever we partake of the Lord's Supper and *eat our way to health and life!*

By the way, after Adam and Eve sinned, their hearts became cold with fear, and they hid themselves when they heard the voice of God in the garden (Gen. 3:10). But as the resurrected Christ walked with the two disciples on the road to Emmaus, their heart burned with love for Jesus (Luke 24:32), and they wanted to stay longer in His presence (Luke 24:29). Our Lord Jesus has restored the relationship with God that was fractured and lost when Adam and Eve fell, and today we don't ever have to be afraid of the Lord. Whatever challenges come our way, we can have the confidence that He is *for* us (Rom. 8:31), and we can come boldly to His throne of grace (Heb. 4:16).

Each time you break bread, may your eyes be opened to *see Jesus,* and may He be made *known* to you. May you become more and more thoroughly acquainted with Him and have a deeper and deeper revelation of His loveliness and perfection. The Communion is all about remembering Him—not His healing, not His miracles, just Jesus *Himself.*

IT IS ALL ABOUT JESUS

By now, you are probably familiar with Isaiah 53:4, which says:

Surely He has borne our griefs and carried our sorrows.

When the author of the gospel of Matthew quoted it, he said:

"He *Himself* took our infirmities and bore our sicknesses." (Matt. 8:17)

I love the word *Himself* because it is so personal and so intimate.

Surely He Himself took our diseases and our infirmities. It wasn't an angel. Your health and wholeness were too important to Him, so He *Himself* bore your every sickness and disease.

Take some time to meditate on the word *Himself.* Take some time to remember the One who suffered and died for you, the One who took your infirmities and bore your sicknesses so you need not bear them. Jesus *Himself* did it because you are so precious to Him.

Whatever condition the doctors have diagnosed you with, Jesus Himself has taken it upon His own body. Don't focus on looking for healing; focus on the Lord Jesus Himself. Focus on the One "who *Himself* bore our sins in His own body on the tree, that we, having died to sins, might live for righteousness—by whose stripes you were healed" (1 Peter 2:24).

Many times when you seek Him and simply

> **REMEMBER THE ONE WHO TOOK YOUR INFIRMITIES AND BORE YOUR SICKNESSES SO YOU NEED NOT BEAR THEM.**

spend time in His presence, your fears and worries just melt away. You find that in His presence, there is shalom-peace. There is healing. There is wholeness. And when you look for your symptoms, you find them *no more.*

Why?

Because you are in the presence of the Healer.

When God told the children of Israel, "I am the LORD who heals you" (Ex. 15:26), He was introducing Himself as *Jehovah Rapha.* He was not saying, "I will give you healing" or "I will provide you health." He was saying I AM your healing, and I AM your health. When you touch Jesus, you touch healing. He does not give healing as though it were a thing. He gives Himself.

WHEN YOU TOUCH JESUS, YOU TOUCH HEALING.

There are many studies that claim to have found the secret to longevity and health, and they tell you all the things you need to eat and do if you want to live long and stay healthy. I have nothing against these studies and fully agree you *should* make healthy food and life-style choices. But when your well-being is dependent on things you need to *do*, you will never be secure. Let your healing and security be based, instead, on someone who never fails, someone who is all-powerful, all-knowing, and best of all, all-loving. That's when you can have security that is unshakable and peace unspeakable.

You don't have to seek after healing, provision, and protection. When you have Jesus, you have all you need. If there is an area of death in your body, the Lord says to you, "*I* am the resurrection and the life" (John 11:25). If doctors have told you that you will die young, the Lord says to you, "*I* am your life and the length of your days" (Deut. 30:20). If you have received a negative diagnosis and are fearful, the Lord says to you, "Do not be afraid. *I* am your shield" (Gen. 15:1). If you have been dealing with relapse after relapse and the discouragement is over-whelming you, the Lord declares to you, "*I* am your strength and your song" (Ex. 15:2)!

LIVE LOVED BY THE SHEPHERD

Whatever you are facing in your life, you don't have to run around trying to meet all your needs. You just need to seek Jesus *Himself.* When you have the person of Jesus, you have all the benefits that come with the person.

Here is one particular aspect of the Lord that I want to draw your attention to.

Throughout the Bible, we see pictures of God. We see Him personified as our fortress, our stronghold, and our tower. But of all the pictures used throughout both the Old and New Testaments, one of the most frequently used is of God as our Shepherd.

WHEN YOU HAVE JESUS, YOU HAVE ALL YOU NEED.

And many times we see the imagery of the shepherd and sheep used in the context of healing.

For instance, it says in Ezekiel:

> "I will feed My flock, and I will make them lie down," says the Lord GOD. "I will seek what was lost and bring back what was driven away, *bind up the broken and strengthen what was sick.*" (Ezek. 34:15–16)

I love wide-margin Bibles because I can write my own commentaries. There are notes written all over my Bible, and next to Isaiah 53:5–6 and 1 Peter 2:24–25, I wrote, "This imagery of Shepherd and flock promotes healing."

Let me show you something really powerful when you compare these two Scripture passages:

> But He was wounded for our transgressions, He was bruised for our iniquities; the chastisement for our peace was upon Him, *and by His stripes we are healed. All we like sheep have gone astray;* we have turned, every one, to his own way; and the LORD has laid on Him the iniquity of us all. (Isa. 53:5–6)

Who Himself bore our sins in His own body on the tree, that we, having died to sins, might live for righteousness—by whose stripes you were healed. For you were like sheep going astray, but have now returned to the Shepherd and Overseer of your souls. (1 Peter 2:24–25)

During my time of study, I felt the Lord say to me, "The day My people see Me as their Shepherd, and not just know it in their heads, but really experience Me as their Shepherd, their days of sickness are over."

We were like sheep going astray, and that's why we were sick. But now we are no longer like sheep that have gone astray. We have *now returned to the Shepherd and Overseer of our souls.* And because of that, we can have full assurance that by His stripes, we are healed.

> **OUR PART AS HIS SHEEP IS TO SIMPLY CONSENT TO BE LOVED BY HIM, LET HIM CARRY US ON HIS SHOULDERS, AND REST IN HIS STRENGTH.**

By the way, the word for *returned* in the original Greek text is in the passive voice.[2] This means you are not the active agent here. It is the Holy Spirit who has brought you back and returned you. Do you remember the parable our Lord Jesus told about the shepherd who left the ninety-nine sheep to look for the one that was lost (Luke 15:1–7)? The Shepherd is the One who looks for the lost sheep, finds it, and lays it on His shoulder, rejoicing. Our part as sheep is to *simply consent to be loved by Him*, let Him carry us on His shoulders, and rest in His strength.

Incidentally, if you look closer at this parable, our Lord Jesus was actually teaching about *repentance*. At the end of the parable, He said, "I say to you that likewise there will be more joy in heaven over one sinner who repents than over ninety-nine just persons who need no repentance" (Luke 15:7). But let me ask you this: What exactly did the sheep do to "repent"? Wasn't it the Shepherd who did everything?

Precisely. Many people think that repentance is about beating themselves up and condemning themselves for their actions. There is a place for an outward expression of remorse, and Jesus talked about such repentance when He said, "Woe to you, Chorazin! Woe to you, Bethsaida! For if the mighty works which were done in you had been done in Tyre and Sidon, they would have repented long ago in sackcloth and ashes" (Matt. 11:21).

But the Greek word used for *repentance* is *metanoia*, and it actually means "a change of mind."[3] This means repentance can take place quietly, without any outward display, and I believe repentance is happening even right now as you read this book and hear truths about how God loves you and is *for* you. In the parable of the lost sheep, the sheep did not *do* anything to "repent." It simply allowed the shepherd to find it and lay it on his shoulders. And that's how our Lord Jesus defines repentance in the new covenant. Repentance is a response to His love. It's you consenting to be saved. Consenting to be loved. Consenting to be carried on His strong shoulders and embraced by His arms of love. That's repentance.

> **REPENTANCE IS YOU RESPONDING TO HIS LOVE AND CONSENTING TO BE SAVED.**

If you used to believe God uses sickness to chastise you or teach you a lesson, or if you used to think you are disqualified from receiving healing, I pray that you have *repented* of such erroneous beliefs, and you now know you have a Shepherd who wants you to rest in His love and strength, a Shepherd who pursues you when you are lost, a Shepherd who rejoices over you when you are found!

YOUR LOVING SHEPHERD SUPPLIES ALL YOUR NEEDS

Another well-known picture of God as our Shepherd is articulated in the beautiful Psalm 23. It was written by David, a shepherd who saw the Lord as his Shepherd:

The LORD is my shepherd;

I shall not want.

He makes me to lie down in green pastures;

He leads me beside the still waters.

He restores my soul;

He leads me in the paths of righteousness

For His name's sake.

Yea, though I walk through the valley of the shadow of death,

I will fear no evil;

For You are with me;

Your rod and Your staff, they comfort me.

You prepare a table before me in the presence of my enemies;

You anoint my head with oil;

My cup runs over.

Surely goodness and mercy shall follow me

All the days of my life;

And I will dwell in the house of the LORD

Forever.

STAY CLOSE TO YOUR GOOD SHEPHERD AND ALLOW HIM TO PROVIDE FOR YOU.

When you see the Lord as your Shepherd, you will not lack, and that includes not lacking for health. Whatever needs you have, you will not lack because your Good Shepherd provides. You don't have to run yourself ragged trying to take care of everything and live as though you have no God. Whatever medical condition you are faced with, whatever bad report you have received, stay close to the Shepherd, and allow Him to provide for you.

REST IN HIS FINISHED WORK

And did you notice the first thing the Shepherd does? The psalmist wrote, "He makes me to *lie down* in green pastures" (Ps. 23:2). When you allow Him to be your Good Shepherd, He will bring you to green pastures and make you lie down. You can rest, for He will provide for you. He will lead you beside still waters where you can drink and be refreshed. The Hebrew word for *still* is *manuka*, which means "rest."[4] He wants you in a place of resting in what He has done, resting in the victory He has already won at the cross.

It is not by coincidence that many of Jesus' healing miracles took place on the Sabbath. He healed a man with a withered hand (Matt. 12:10–13), a woman bowed down for eighteen years (Luke 13:10–13), a man with dropsy (Luke 14:2–4), and another man with a thirty-eight-year infirmity at the pool of Bethesda (John 5:2–9), all on the Sabbath. God told His people to observe the Sabbath as a day of rest (Ex. 20:8–11). When we rest, God works; when we work, God rests. I don't know about you, but I can't afford not to have God working in every area in my life!

Maybe you or your loved ones have been dealing with a chronic condition. Allow me to explain that "rest" does not mean you don't do anything. It doesn't mean you don't do what your doctors have advised, you don't carry out the physiotherapy exercises prescribed to you, and you simply sit at home in denial.

> REST IS NOT INACTIVITY; IT IS SPIRIT-DIRECTED ACTIVITY.

Rest is *not* inactivity; it is Spirit-directed activity where you allow the Holy Spirit to lead you in what to do, and you do it without worrying because you know He is in control.

Do you want to know the result of allowing the Lord to give us rest? Let me show you what King Solomon said:

> But now the LORD my God has given me rest on every side; there is neither adversary nor evil occurrence. (1 Kings 5:4)

Don't you love that? I pray that you will experience that in Jesus' name—to come to a place where there is neither adversary nor evil occurrence in your life. Amen!

Beloved, today I pray that you will see this. You don't have to try

LIVE LIFE LOVED BY YOUR GOOD SHEPHERD, KNOWING HE WATCHES OVER YOU.

to handle everything and be in control of everything in your life. God never meant for you to be your own savior. God is our Good Shepherd, and He wants you to live life loved by Him, knowing that He watches over you. You don't have to keep looking out for yourself and live life as though you don't have a God.

Even if you find yourself walking through the valley of the shadow of death, you can fear no evil, for your Good Shepherd *is* with you. Some years ago, I saw for myself how the Lord brought someone through the valley of the shadow of death and literally brought her back from death to life through the holy Communion.

BROUGHT BACK TO LIFE

For years we had been organizing trips to Israel for the people in our church. One day we were informed there had been an emergency. One of the ladies from our church had just landed in Tel Aviv. As she was disembarking from the plane, she suddenly collapsed and started foaming at the mouth. An ambulance was immediately dispatched, but on the way to the Assaf Harofeh Medical Center, she suffered a cardiac arrest and her heart stopped. At the hospital, the doctors tried to save her, but there was no response and they almost gave up. Fortunately, they managed to resuscitate her. They were only able to keep her alive through life support, however, and her condition remained critical.

Her doctors diagnosed her with deep vein thrombosis, a rare condition that develops when a blood clot is formed in a vein deep in the body. During the flight, a clot had formed in her leg, traveled to her heart and finally to one of her lungs. They warned that she would not be able to survive, and even if she did, her brain had been deprived of oxygen for too long. Her doctors monitored her closely, fearing her condition would deteriorate even further.

The lady's husband and some of her family members who were with her prayed over her and partook of the Communion, declaring health and wholeness over her. The church leaders in charge of her tour group also prayed over her.

Meanwhile, my pastors and I were elsewhere in Israel, and by the time we got to the hospital, her face was all bloated and she was hooked up to various tubes and medical instruments. One of my pastors shared with me later that she was in such a dismal condition that he could not look at her. He had to close his eyes when he prayed for her. In the natural, it was really hard to believe she would recover. But by faith, we partook of the Communion in the intensive care unit together with her family and declared that, by the broken body of our Lord Jesus, life was being released into her.

The very next day, she regained consciousness. And her doctors could not find a trace of any clot.

They could not understand where the clot had gone. They called her recovery a "miracle" and insisted on keeping her under observation for a few days. But we knew what had happened. Our Lord Jesus had healed her and removed the clot!

And guess what the lady did when she was discharged? She joined the next tour group from our church, and the first place she visited was the Garden Tomb, the place where our Lord Jesus was raised from the dead. Hallelujah!

HAVE YOU FALLEN INTO A PIT?

Our Lord Jesus went into a synagogue on the Sabbath, and a man was there with a withered hand. The Pharisees were looking for opportunities to accuse Jesus of wrongdoing, so they challenged Him, saying, "Is it lawful to heal on the Sabbath?" Our Lord answered, "What man is there among you who has one sheep, and if it falls into a pit on the Sabbath, will not lay hold of it and lift it out? Of how much more value then is a man than a sheep? Therefore it is lawful to do good on the Sabbath." Then He said to the man, "Stretch out your hand." And he stretched it out, and it was restored as whole as the other (Matt. 12:9–13).

This is what I want you to know: when someone is sick, the Lord never faults and condemns the person. He sees the person as a sheep that has fallen into a pit, a sheep that is in need of rescuing. If you are dealing with a medical condition, don't allow the accuser to disqualify you from receiving your healing by telling you things like, "You should have watched your diet" or "You should have exercised more." Even if you were at fault, the Lord Jesus can heal you, and He is most willing to.

> JESUS NEVER CONDEMNS YOU WHEN YOU ARE SICK; HE SEES YOU IN NEED OF RESCUING.

That doesn't mean you neglect wisdom in taking care of your health. If you allow Him to, the Lord can lead you even in practical matters like what to eat and how to exercise. The key here is not to pay attention to the voice of shame, condemnation, and accusation. Listen instead to the voice of your Shepherd coming to rescue you!

THE GOOD SHEPHERD LAYS DOWN HIS LIFE FOR HIS SHEEP

The Bible tells us that the Good Shepherd gives His life for the sheep (John 10:11). But do you know the context of this verse? Let me show you:

> "The thief does not come except to steal, and to kill, and to destroy. I have come that they may have life, and that they may have it more abundantly. I am the good shepherd. The good shepherd gives His life for the sheep." (John 10:10–11)

Even though He is our Shepherd, He laid down His life as the Lamb of God. Revelation 5:12 declares, "Worthy is the *Lamb* who was slain." Why does God use the picture of the Lamb and not the Shepherd in the sacrifice? Because God wants you to see that Jesus died in *your* place. He, the Good Shepherd, became the Lamb of God for you. You can have life more abundantly not because you deserve it but because He gave His life for yours. He took your sicknesses and your pains, and gave you His wholeness and His health.

> YOU CAN HAVE LIFE MORE ABUNDANTLY BECAUSE HE GAVE HIS LIFE FOR YOURS.

Therefore, "do not fear, little flock, for it is your Father's good pleasure to give you the kingdom" (Luke 12:32). Do not fear. Whatever condition you might be faced with, you can believe you will see the full manifestation of your healing. Keep partaking of the Tree of Life and allow His abundant life to flood your body each time you partake. God has already given you the best that heaven has—the Lord Jesus Himself. How will He not with Jesus also *freely give you all things* (Rom. 8:32)? Whatever you might be facing, do not lose heart. You *will* "see the goodness of the LORD in the land of the living" (Ps. 27:13)!

CLOSING WORDS

I pray this book has strengthened and encouraged you, and that you now know beyond the shadow of a doubt that God wants you and your loved ones healed and well.

I also hope you have learned how you can come boldly to His table and eat and drink of the Lord's supernatural healing, health, wholeness, and life through the holy Communion.

You can partake of the holy Communion by yourself. But I want to encourage you to partake of the Communion together with your family or with like-minded believers who can surround you with faith, especially when you have no strength to believe for yourself. When you gather in His name, He promised in His Word that He will be in your midst (Matt. 18:20). Don't take this journey alone.

For now, would you give me the privilege of partaking of the Communion together with you? Please prepare the elements of the Communion, and when you are ready, read on.

Let's hold the bread in our hands and talk to our Healer, who paid the price for our health and wholeness at the cross of Calvary:

Dear Lord Jesus, we come to You, and we remember all that You have done for us on the cross. Thank You for loving us so much

You gave up heaven for us. Thank You for allowing Your body to be broken so that ours might be whole. As we partake, we receive Your resurrection life, health, and strength. By Your grace, we shall be completely strong and healthy all the days of our lives. Our eyes shall not grow dim, nor shall our strength be abated. No sickness can remain in our bodies because the same power that raised You from the grave flows through us. By Your stripes, we are healed.

Let's partake of the bread.

Now hold the cup in your hands and tell Him:

Lord Jesus, thank You for Your precious blood. Thank You for washing us clean of all our sins. We stand before You completely righteous and forgiven. Your blood has redeemed us from every curse, and today we can freely receive all the blessings that crown the head of the righteous!

Let's drink.

Right now, I believe you are already stronger and healthier. Hallelujah!

I am looking forward to hearing from you when you receive your breakthrough. When that happens, would you write to me at JosephPrince.com/eat so that together we can encourage others who are still trusting God for the manifestation of their healing?

My friend, you are so loved.

I pray that even as you close this book, the Lord has already left an indelible deposit in your heart and that you have experienced His personal love for you in a way you never thought possible. May you continue to see in all the Scriptures the things concerning Himself. And may you come to His table often, seizing each opportunity to remember all He has done for you and to proclaim His finished work. I declare that your healthiest, most robust, and most energetic days are ahead of you, in Jesus' name! Amen.

FREQUENTLY ASKED QUESTIONS ABOUT THE HOLY COMMUNION

I pray that what I have shared in the preceding chapters has anchored your heart more and more in the Lord's love for you. I pray that you have come to see how much He wants you healed and well, how much He suffered to purchase your healing, and how receiving the holy Communion is His simple but powerful way for you to walk in His healing, wholeness, and abundant life.

My friend, healing is a grace gift. This means God has done it all. You only have to thank Him for it and receive it. And that is what the Communion is about—receiving what He has already done for you.

If you had questions that kept you from fully partaking of the Communion as the apostle Paul and the early church did, I hope I have answered them. If I have not, I hope to address them here. May these answers settle your heart, cause you to really lay hold of this grace gift, and launch you on a wonderful journey of seeing His healing made real in your life and in the lives of your loved ones.

1. How often can I partake of the holy Communion?

You can partake of the holy Communion and receive the full benefits of the finished work of Christ as often as you want. Our Lord Jesus said, "This do, as often as you drink it, in remembrance of Me" (1 Cor. 11:25). Notice He said "as often," not "as seldom"!

Our Lord Jesus doesn't limit the number of times you can draw from Him. His supply is inexhaustible, and I pray that He will increase your revelation of His love for you and expand your capacity to receive from Him. When He multiplied five loaves and two fish to feed five thousand people, His supply did not stop until the people had taken "as much as they wanted" (John 6:11). The supply did not stop because He ran out of bread and fish. It stopped because the people had eaten enough. And still, there were "twelve large baskets" of leftovers (John 6:13 AMP).

Can you see how extravagant the Lord is toward you, and how His heart desires to bless and heal you? He doesn't want you to take from Him with a timid hand when His heart is so lavish toward you. He wants to pour out His blessings upon you, and He wants you to receive every blessing of health, wholeness, and long life that He died to give you.

If you are being attacked by symptoms throughout the day, I want to encourage you to partake of the Communion throughout the day. If the enemy is attacking you day and night, then lift up the bread and cup day and night and partake of His finished work day and night. If you have been prescribed medication that comes with certain side effects, don't take just the medication. Partake of the Communion every time you take your medication, and trust Him to protect you from the medication's side effects.

Whether your medication is taken once or three times a day, partake of the Communion elements as well in faith, and each time thank Him. Each time, declare that by His stripes, you are healed (Isa. 53:5). Declare that with long life He will satisfy you and show you His salvation (Ps. 91:16). Say boldly, "The Lord forgives all my iniquities and heals all my diseases. I shall not die but live and declare His goodness toward me!" (Ps. 103:3; 118:17).

2. Must only unleavened matzah bread and grape juice be used? Can I use ordinary bread and even water? What about using wine?

Partaking of the holy Communion isn't about putting a particular kind of bread in your mouth or swallowing a particular concoction. The power of the Communion does not lie in the physical ingredients of the bread or drink. There is no special recipe to adhere to. The elements have nothing to do with the kind of flour or liquid used, number of calories they contain, or nutritional value they offer.

If you are able to get hold of the Jewish matzah bread I talked about in chapter 2, then you can use that. But it certainly does not mean you cannot partake of the Communion if you don't have matzah bread. You can use any bread or cracker you have at home. There are even crackers that are pierced, striped, and burnt like the matzah bread. These will help to remind you of what the Lord Jesus has done for you.

As for the cup, if you can, take something like grape juice that is the "fruit of the vine" (Luke 22:18) to remind you of your Savior's precious blood that was shed for you.

Some people have written in to ask about using wine. In our church and care groups, we do *not* use wine because there may be a few people who have a weakness for alcohol. As taught by the apostle Paul, we do not want to cause anyone to stumble (1 Cor. 8:13). And knowing that individuals have different thresholds for alcohol, we want to avoid the possibility of anyone getting drunk.

God is clearly against drunkenness (Rom. 13:13; Eph. 5:18), and that was one of the reasons Paul had to correct the Corinthian Christians who were getting drunk on wine during the Lord's Supper (1 Cor. 11:21). So if you have a weakness for alcohol or are recovering from an alcohol addiction, then as a matter of wisdom, I would suggest you use a non-alcoholic drink such as grape juice, which is easily available.

If you plan to partake of the Communion regularly, for example, on a daily basis, then consider gathering the elements you want to use and having them prepared and ready. If you don't have the recommended elements with you but feel led to partake of the Lord's Supper, you can use any bread or biscuit and plain water. It is not about what type of bread or drink to use; it is about remembering the finished work of our Lord and Savior, Jesus Christ.

We have received many testimonies from people who experienced healing as they partook of the Communion in faith, even though all they used were biscuits and plain water. Many of these precious folks felt led to partake of the Communion while they were in a hospital. Some had just rushed their children to the hospital; some, sent by their specialist doctors, were waiting to go for further testing. Armed with a revelation of the Communion, they used whatever type of bread or crackers they could get their hands on. In like manner, if they couldn't find grape juice, they used plain water.

With just those simple elements, they remembered the Lord's finished work on the cross and received the Communion. Later, they wrote to my ministry to tell how they saw the Lord deliver them or their loved ones from high fevers and even tumors, or how they saw the Lord accelerate their recovery from strokes or other medical conditions.

Isn't the Lord so good? My friend, the Communion is all about Him and His *finished* work. This means there is nothing you can do by your own efforts that will make the Communion more holy or effective. All you need to do is come and partake. And even if you can only get hold of ordinary bread and water, you can still partake in faith and receive the Lord's healing.

3. Is it okay for me to partake of the holy Communion on my own at home, rather than in a church where an ordained pastor or church leader ministers it to me?

Many people fear partaking of the holy Communion on their own at home because they have been taught, or assume after having partaken of the Communion in church, that only a qualified pastor can minister the elements and this should be done in a church. They may even have been taught that to do it on their own is to invite punishment from God.

Nowhere in Scripture do you find these conditions and prohibitions.

What you do find is that on the night Jesus instituted the holy Communion, He said *directly* to His beloved disciples, "Do this often in remembrance of Me" (1 Cor. 11:24–25). And He didn't add, "But make sure you get a qualified pastor to do it for you, and do it in a church." If Jesus didn't give these conditions, why would we want to add to His words?

If you are still concerned about not being "qualified," then let me show you just how perfectly qualified you are, not through anything you have done but through what the Lord Jesus has done for you.

The Bible says that Jesus "loved us and washed us from our sins in His own blood, and *has made us kings and priests* to His God and Father" (Rev. 1:5–6; 5:10). Christ has made you not just a king but also a priest.

Beloved, you are a priest to God, fully qualified by the Lord Jesus who has washed from you all your sins with His own blood. If Jesus Himself has qualified you to be a priest to God, surely you have the blood-bought right to partake of the Communion on your own.

You are also a priest to your family, to your children. You have the God-given anointing and authority to pray for them, to bring them up in the ways of God (Prov. 22:6), and also to minister the holy Communion to them. Jesus paid a heavy price for you to have this position of authority and influence, so never apologize for it or take it lightly.

What about partaking of the meal in the comfort of your own home?

Scripture tells us the early church *"met in homes for the Lord's Supper,* and shared their meals with great joy and generosity" (Acts 2:46 NLT). They partook of the Communion in their own homes. If you think about it, how else were they going to partake *often* as instructed by the Lord?

Today many churches have Communion only once or twice a month or on special occasions like Good Friday. But how can you partake often if you are to partake only at those times and in a church? Of course you can invite your pastor over to minister to you the Communion, especially if you are too sick to travel to church. However, if you want to partake of the Communion, say two or three times a day when you take your medication, can you see how impractical it would be if your pastor or church leader needed to be there each time to minister it to you?

My friend, our God is a loving and practical God, and if He invites you to His table, He doesn't place obstacles in your way. His table of grace is not encumbered with restrictions. Christ has qualified you to partake on your own, and it is not so much *where* you partake of the Communion as it is with *whom* you partake.

The Lord's Supper is a special meal in which you have intimate communion with your Savior, remembering with thankfulness all He has done for you. And you can certainly do that not just in church on Sundays but also at home, in your hotel room, or even in your hospital room, any time of the day, any day of the week.

4. Will the holy Communion "work" if the one partaking of it is not a believer of Jesus?

What we need to understand is that simply ingesting the elements of the holy Communion will not yield results. In and of themselves, there is nothing special or magical about the elements of the holy Communion.

The Communion is a time of intimacy with the Lord, a time when you remember His love for you. It is when you partake of the elements with *revelation*—seeing His body broken for you as you break the bread in your hands, and seeing His blood shed for you as you drink of the cup—that His power is released to heal and deliver you from sickness and disease. This is why in our church, we invite only believers to partake of the Communion during our services. Without revelation and relationship, the Communion would just be an empty ritual to nonbelievers.

I have shared extensively about this in chapter 7 and want to encourage you to read the chapter again to fully understand why the power of the Communion is based on a personal *revelation* of His love and faith in His finished work.

But if you have nonbelieving relatives, friends, colleagues, or neighbors who might be facing medical challenges, please go ahead and pray for them, and let them know you are talking to the Lord for them. In your own time with the Lord, you can partake of the Communion on their behalf and believe with them for their breakthrough. You are the righteousness of God in Christ and God hears your prayers (2 Cor. 5:21; Prov. 15:29). The Bible even says the prayer of a righteous person "has great power and produces wonderful results" (James 5:16 NLT).

By all means, share the gospel with them if the Lord opens the door for you to do so, but don't worry about whether they are believers or not at this point. Just make sure they know you are praying for them so that when they are healed they will know it is the Lord who healed them!

Share with them the testimonies you have read in this book, and tell them there is a God of miracles who can heal them and is most willing to. Tell them they don't have to handle their challenges all by themselves, because God loves them and wants to help them in their times of need.

They *do not* have to receive Christ as their Lord and Savior for God to heal them. Did you realize that none of the people whom Jesus healed during His earthly ministry were "Christians" to begin with, since He had not gone to the cross yet? And interestingly, in the very first mention of healing in the Bible, righteous Abraham prayed for the heathen king Abimelech, "and God healed Abimelech," and not just him, but also "his wife, and his female servants" (Gen. 20:17).

In the same way, just because your friends are not believers does not disqualify them from the Lord's healing. It is the goodness and kindness of God that melts our hearts and leads us to repentance (Rom. 2:4). It is not our repentance that leads us to God's goodness. When they experience His goodness and His healing power for themselves, I believe they will want to know Him more.

There is a promise in Acts 16:31 that declares, "Believe on the Lord Jesus Christ, and you will be saved, *you and your household*." What does that mean?

God loves your nonbelieving family members, too, and He wants every one of them saved. Even under the old covenant, God told the children of Israel to take a lamb for the whole household (Ex. 12:3). This does not mean that once you believe in Jesus, your family members are automatically saved. But when you received Jesus, the Lamb of God, as your Lord and Savior, you opened a big door for Him to move into and touch the lives of your family members.

The word *saved* is translated from the Greek word *sozo*, which means "to save, heal, preserve, and rescue."[1] The greatest blessing for your family members is for them to invite Jesus into their lives as their Lord and Savior and to know once and for all that their sins have been washed away and heaven is their home.

But on the cross, Jesus did not just bear their sins; He also bore their sicknesses. If you have family members who are in a hospital or battling a disease right now, I pray that the Lord will create opportunities for you to pray for them and to share with them all that Jesus has done for them. Get ready for them to be saved, healed, preserved, and rescued!

5. Can my young child partake of the holy Communion if he or she doesn't fully understand what it is about?

As a parent myself, I am so glad to know our children have a special place in the Lord's heart. When He saved us, He had our children in mind too (Acts 16:31).

What do I mean by this? The Lord's blessings on a person always include blessings on that person's children and family life (Deut. 11:21; 28:4 NLT; Isa. 54:13; Ps. 127:1–5; 128:3–5). In chapter 3, we saw how the blood of the Passover lamb that the Israelites applied on the doorposts and lintel covered *the whole family* (children and all) inside the house.

My friend, God wants you to be at rest, knowing without a doubt that His finished work and healing and protection promises cover your children too (Ps. 91:10).

May I show you one more thing? I want you to see God's heart regarding children. In the gospel of Luke, when some parents "brought infants to Him that He might touch them," His disciples saw what the parents were doing and promptly rebuked them (Luke 18:15). Our Lord Jesus stopped His disciples, then "called [the children] to Him" and said, "*Let the little children come to Me, and do not forbid them*; for of such is the kingdom of God" (Luke 18:16). Isn't that beautiful?

A wonderful way to bring your young children to Jesus is to bring them to the Lord's Table—as often as *you* partake of the Communion. They don't have to be sick to join you in partaking of the Communion. If they were, it would be awesome if they could partake of the Communion with you too.

You can keep it simple and personal and tell them, "Do you know how much Daddy (or Mommy) loves you? Jesus loves you so much too. Let's say 'thank You' to Him, shall we?"

Then you can take the bread, give it to them, and say, "Let's talk to Jesus, okay? Thank You, Jesus, for loving [mention each family member partaking]. Thank You for keeping us healthy and well. When we are sick, You are our healer. You love us and always want us happy. Thank You for fixing what is hurting in our bodies. Thank You for keeping us well. Amen." Then lead them to eat the bread.

Then take the cup and pray, "Lord Jesus, thank You for always loving us and taking care of us. Thank You for being our best friend. Thank You for forgiving us. With You, we never have to be afraid. Whatever we need, You understand. Because You went to the cross and died for us, we have everything we need to be happy, healthy, and well. Thank You, Jesus. Amen." Then lead them to drink the juice.

It's really as simple as that. I believe that as you actively bring your children into the Lord's presence through the Communion this way, you and they will see the Lord being faithful to those words you have prayed. You will see the Lord Himself guard their bodies, spirits, minds, and emotions with His all-encompassing shalom-peace (Isa. 54:13).

As a parent, you are the spiritual authority in your children's lives, and to you belongs the privilege of bringing them to the Lord and pointing them to His love for them. In Deuteronomy 11:19, the Lord exhorts us as parents to teach His Word to our children, "speaking of them [scriptures] when you sit in your house, when you walk by the way, when you lie down, and when you rise up." Why?

So that through the Word they will come to see His perfect love for them, and you and your children may live good, long lives and experience days of heaven on earth (Deut. 11:21). When you partake of the Communion with them, are you not teaching them about the Lord and pointing them to His love? Then as His Word in Deuteronomy 11:21 promises, you and your children will experience here on earth days of heaven (where there is no sickness) and long life.

Dear reader, as you see how easy the Lord has made it for you and your loved ones to receive His divine healing, strength, and life, I pray that you will seize every opportunity to come to the Lord's Table and partake of the elements. I am believing with you that as you partake, you will become stronger and healthier. I declare that according to His Word, you will *not* remain sick or die, but live and see the goodness of the Lord in the land of the living (Ps. 27:13). You and your loved ones *will* experience length of days and the abundant life that are yours and theirs in Christ!

APPENDIX

Key Greek Words Used and Their Meanings in 1 Corinthians 11:28–32

As I promised in chapter 1, allow me to provide a detailed explanation of the key Greek words used in 1 Corinthians 11:28–32. I believe an understanding of these words will clear up doubts and fears you may have concerning God punishing believers with sickness and death if they partake of the Communion in a "wrong" way.

How does an understanding of Greek words help us? Greek is such a rich language that one word may have numerous meanings. For example, the English words *judge* and *judgment* used many times in this passage (and that cause a lot of fear in believers) actually translate into different Greek words, each with their own meanings. In fact, the Greek word for *judge*, *krino*, has seven different meanings, much like the word *love* in English, which can include the meanings of affection, attraction, admiration, devotion, loyalty (and even a zero score in tennis!), and can be applied to humans as well as physical objects. As such, knowing which original Greek word was used, and which meaning of that word was intended by the author, is crucial to arriving at an accurate understanding of the passage as a whole.

So let me show you the meanings of the key Greek words used in 1 Corinthians 11:29–32, how they reveal to us that God does *not* punish, judge, or chasten His children with sickness and death, and how they actually apply to you, the believer.

Let's start with verse 28: "Let a man examine himself." The word *examine* is the Greek word *dokimazo* (Strong's #1381), which *Vine's Expository Dictionary of Biblical Words* defines as "to prove with a view to approving" or "to approve, deem worthy." To examine yourself is to know God approves of you partaking and receiving what Jesus suffered to give you. When you partake of the Communion, you are examining yourself rightly when you say, "I know the purpose of the Lord's Supper. I know His body was broken for my sicknesses, and I partake receiving His health. I'm approving what He has already approved."

Can you see? To examine yourself does not mean to check yourself for sins committed. Notice that verse 28 says, "Let a man examine himself, and so let him eat of the bread and drink of the cup." It does not say, "Let a man examine himself for sin and abstain from the bread and the cup." In fact, to partake with sin-consciousness after all the Lord has done to secure our forgiveness and healing is to partake "in an unworthy manner," and according to verse 29, such a believer "eats and drinks judgment to himself."

Judgment in the Greek is *krima* (Strong's #2917), which means "condemnation of wrong." The reflexive pronoun *himself* indicates that *this believer* (not God) is performing the judgment upon himself. *He* is condemning himself when he partakes with self-condemnation and sin-consciousness. To partake like that is to partake unworthily, because the cup is proof that the blood of Christ has remitted the believer's sins, yet he is still seeing them on himself.

Partaking with sin-consciousness is also "not discerning the Lord's body" (v. 29). The word *discerning* is *diakrino* (Strong's #1252), which *Thayer's Greek Lexicon* defines as "to separate, make a distinction." Here, the apostle Paul is talking about the believer who fails to make the distinction that Christ's body has borne his sins and sicknesses so that he can be separated from the world and not suffer what the world (nonbelievers) suffers—condemnation, weakness, sickness, and premature death.

Many believers don't make a distinction between the bread and the cup. They lump the two together when they partake of the Communion, very likely because they have not been taught that the Lord's body was broken for theirs to be whole and how to discern His body when they partake. As I shared in chapter 1, failure to discern this about the Lord's body is the singular reason given by the apostle Paul as to why many in the church are weak, sick, and dying prematurely (v. 30).

Paul adds that if we would "judge [*diakrino*] ourselves"—as distinct from the people of the world and set apart to receive the benefits of the Lord's body broken for us—then we would not "be judged" by God (v. 31). Many believers immediately understand this to mean damnation by God, but this is where it is useful to know that the Greek word for *judged* is *krino* (Strong's #2919) and that it has seven different meanings according to *Vine's Expository Dictionary of Biblical Words.*

While *krino* can certainly mean eternal condemnation by the courts of heaven, this cannot be the meaning intended here, because Scripture says clearly that "he who believes in Him is not condemned [*krino*]" (John 3:18). Rather, the intended meaning of *krino* in verse 31 is actually "to subject to censure." In other words, if we would have the right opinion of ourselves as forgiven, righteous, and healed based on our Lord Jesus' finished work, we would not come under God's censure. We would not be corrected, rebuked, or chastened by our heavenly Father.

This is consistent with what Paul states in the next verse: "But when we are judged [*krino*], we are chastened by the Lord" (v. 32). *Chastened* here is the Greek word *paideuo* (Strong's #3811), and it means "to train children." How does God, our heavenly Father, chasten or train us, His children? Does He do it through making us sick or causing accidents to happen to us? Absolutely not. God chastens us through His Spirit and His Word (Heb. 12:9–10).

Paul tells us in 2 Timothy 3:16 that God's Word is profitable "for reproof, for correction, for instruction in righteousness." There is a profiting in His censuring and correcting that we may live and be partakers of His holiness (Heb. 12:9–10). *That we may live* would not be possible if His chastening is sickness or accidents that lead to death. Notice that the way the Corinthian believers were censured for their disorderly behavior when they came together to partake of the Communion was through Paul bringing a fresh word of the Communion to them.

God chastens us because we are His children and He loves us (Heb. 12:6). He does not want us to be "condemned with the world" (v. 32), but to truly understand the difference the cross of Jesus has made in our lives, so that there is a "clear distinction" between His people and the people of the world, as was the case when He made a difference between the Israelites and Egyptians (Ex. 8:23; 11:7 NLT).

The holy Communion is therefore His provision for His children to be distinct from the world and not be "condemned with the world." The word *condemned* is *katakrino* (Strong's #2632), meaning to "pass sentence upon." In this context, *katakrino* refers to a divine sentence of weakness, sickness, and death that was passed upon the world when Adam sinned.

The present world we live in is a fallen one, where all are subject to weaknesses, sicknesses, and afflictions of the body and mind. But as children of God, we need not be condemned with the world. We can be distinct from nonbelievers of the world, and live strong, healthy, and long, if we would discern the Lord's body, and discern how we are *in Him*. In Him, we are forgiven, made righteous, and completely qualified to partake of the Communion and of the healing and wholeness He has purchased for us on the cross.

I pray what you have read here has helped to clarify any doubts you might have regarding the holy Communion. But whether you understand all the Greek words or not, because you are a believer in Christ Jesus, you *can* partake of the holy Communion without sin-consciousness and fear. You can partake of the Communion with faith and confidence. Because of His finished work, you can freely receive through the Communion every blessing the Lord Jesus died to give you, including healing, health, and wholeness.

(The meanings of various Greek words are taken from *Biblesoft's New Exhaustive Strong's Numbers and Concordance with Expanded Greek-Hebrew Dictionary*, *The Online Bible Thayer's Greek Lexicon*, and *Vine's Expository Dictionary of Biblical Words*.)

NOTES

Introduction

1. Lisa Rabasca Roepe, "The Diet Industry," *SAGE Business Researcher*, March 5, 2018, http://businessresearcher.sagepub.com/sbr-1946 -105904-2881576/20180305/the-diet-industry.

Chapter 1: Come to the Table

1. NT: 1252, Joseph Henry Thayer, *Thayer's Greek Lexicon* (electronic database). Copyright © 2000, 2003, 2006 by Biblesoft, Inc. All rights reserved.

Chapter 2: Not Another Diet Plan

1. "Obesity and Overweight," Centers for Disease Control and Prevention, last reviewed June 13, 2016, https://www.cdc.gov/nchs/fastats/obesity -overweight.htm.
2. "What Are the Consequences?," PublicHealth, accessed February 7, 2019, https://www.publichealth.org/public-awareness/obesity /consequences/.
3. Dan Ledger and Daniel McCaffrey, "Inside Wearables: How the Science of Human Behavior Change Offers the Secret to Long-Term Engagement," Endeavour Partners Archive, January 2014, https:// medium.com/@endeavourprtnrs/inside-wearable-how-the-science-of -human-behavior-change-offers-the-secret-to-long-term-engagement -a15b3c7d4cf3.

4. NT: 2222, William Edwy Vine, *Vine's Expository Dictionary of Biblical Words*. Copyright © 1985, Thomas Nelson Publishers.

5. NT: 5315, James Strong, *Biblesoft's New Exhaustive Strong's Numbers and Concordance of the Bible with Expanded Greek-Hebrew Dictionary*. Copyright © 1994, 2003, 2006 Biblesoft, Inc. and International Bible Translators, Inc.

6. NT: 5176, Joseph Henry Thayer, *Thayer's Greek Lexicon* (electronic database). Copyright © 2000, 2003, 2006 by Biblesoft, Inc. All rights reserved.

7. "A Guide to Shechita," Shechita UK, May 2009, https://www.shechitauk .org/wp-content/uploads/2016/02/A_Guide_to_Shechita_2009__01.pdf.

8. T. J. McCrossan, *Bodily Healing and the Atonement* (Tulsa, OK: Kenneth Hagin Ministries, Inc., 1989), http://www.schoolofgreatness.net /wp-content/uploads/2018/08/Kenneth-E-Hagin-Bodily-Healing-and -Atonement.pdf.

9. Flavius Josephus, *The Wars of the Jews* (Overland Park, KS: Digireads Publishing, 2010).

10. OT: 7291: James Strong, *Biblesoft's New Exhaustive Strong's Numbers and Concordance*.

Chapter 3: None Feeble, None Sick

1. Steve Rudd, "The Exodus Route, the Population of the Exodus Jews, the Number of the Exodus, How Many Hebrews Were in the Exodus," accessed February 14, 2019, http://www.bible.ca/archeology/bible -archeology-exodus-route-population-of-jews-hebrews.htm.

Chapter 4: For You, Not Against You

1. NT: 2222, William Edwy Vine, *Vine's Expository Dictionary of Biblical Words*. Copyright © 1985, Thomas Nelson Publishers.

2. OT: 3444, Joseph Henry Thayer, Francis Brown, Samuel Rolles Driver, and Charles Augustus Briggs, *The Online Bible Thayer's Greek Lexicon and Brown Driver & Briggs Hebrew Lexicon*. Copyright © 1993, Woodside Bible Fellowship, Ontario, Canada. Licensed from the Institute for Creation Research.

Chapter 5: No Place for Fear

1. To read encouraging praise reports about the Lord's love and faithfulness, visit https://blog.JosephPrince.com/category/praise-reports/.

2. Kathryn Watson, "Routine Hair Shedding: Why It Happens and How

Much to Expect," Healthline, accessed January 4, 2019, https://www
.healthline.com/health/how-much-hair-loss-is-normal.

3. "Treatments," Alzheimer's Association, accessed January 4, 2019,
https://www.alz.org/alzheimers-dementia/treatments.

Chapter 6: He Paid the Bill

1. Irene Papanicolas, Liana R. Woskie, and Ashish K. Jha, "Health Care
Spending in the United States and Other High-Income Countries," *Journal
of the American Medical Association*, 319, no. 10 (2018): 1024–39, https://
doi.org/10.1001/jama.2018.1150.

2. "National Health Expenditure Data: Historical," Centers for Medicare
& Medicaid Services, accessed January 7, 2019, https://www.cms.gov
/Research-Statistics-Data-and-Systems/Statistics-Trends-and-Reports
/NationalHealthExpendData/NationalHealthAccountsHistorical
.html.

Chapter 7: Revelation Brings Results

1. OT: 5027, James Strong, *Biblesoft's New Exhaustive Strong's Numbers
and Concordance of the Bible with Expanded Greek-Hebrew Dictionary.*
Copyright © 1994, 2003, 2006 Biblesoft, Inc. and International Bible
Translators, Inc.

2. NT: 40, Joseph Henry Thayer, *Thayer's Greek Lexicon* (electronic database).
Copyright © 2000, 2003, 2006 by Biblesoft, Inc. All rights reserved.

3. NT: 2842, Joseph Henry Thayer, *Thayer's Greek Lexicon.*

4. NT: 4372, Joseph Henry Thayer, *Thayer's Greek Lexicon.*

Chapter 8: Completely Covered, No Exclusions

1. OT: 5315, Joseph Henry Thayer, Francis Brown, Samuel Rolles Driver,
and Charles Augustus Briggs, *The Online Bible Thayer's Greek Lexicon
and Brown Driver & Briggs Hebrew Lexicon.* Copyright © 1993, Woodside Bible Fellowship, Ontario, Canada. Licensed from the Institute for
Creation Research.

2. "What Is Hermatidrosis?," WebMD, last reviewed February 15, 2018,
https://www.webmd.com/a-to-z-guides/hematidrosis-hematohidrosis#1.

Chapter 9: Don't Give Up!

1. NT: 2168, James Strong, *Biblesoft's New Exhaustive Strong's Numbers and
Concordance of the Bible with Expanded Greek-Hebrew Dictionary.* Copyright
© 1994, 2003, 2006 Biblesoft, Inc. and International Bible Translators, Inc.

Chapter 10: The Fight to Rest

1. OT: 4832, James Strong, *Biblesoft's New Exhaustive Strong's Numbers and Concordance of the Bible with Expanded Greek-Hebrew Dictionary.* Copyright © 1994, 2003, 2006 Biblesoft, Inc. and International Bible Translators, Inc.
2. NT: 4982, Joseph Henry Thayer, *Thayer's Greek Lexicon* (electronic database). Copyright © 2000, 2003, 2006 by Biblesoft, Inc. All rights reserved.
3. "The Roman Scourge," Bible History Online, accessed March 4, 2019, https://www.bible-history.com/past/flagrum.html.

Chapter 11: God of Your Valleys

1. NT: 1411, James Strong, *Biblesoft's New Exhaustive Strong's Numbers and Concordance of the Bible with Expanded Greek-Hebrew Dictionary.* Copyright © 1994, 2003, 2006 Biblesoft, Inc. and International Bible Translators, Inc.
2. "Shalem," The NAS Old Testament Hebrew Lexicon, accessed March 11, 2019, https://www.biblestudytools.com/lexicons/hebrew/nas/shalem.html.
3. "Qadar," The NAS Old Testament Hebrew Lexicon.
4. OT: 1298, Joseph Henry Thayer, Francis Brown, Samuel Rolles Driver, and Charles Augustus Briggs, *The Online Bible Thayer's Greek Lexicon and Brown Driver & Briggs Hebrew Lexicon.* Copyright © 1993, Woodside Bible Fellowship, Ontario, Canada. Licensed from the Institute for Creation Research.

Chapter 12: Pursue the Healer

1. NT: 1921, Joseph Henry Thayer, *Thayer's Greek Lexicon* (electronic database). Copyright © 2000, 2003, 2006 by Biblesoft, Inc. All rights reserved.
2. "1 Peter 2:25," BibleHub, accessed March 18, 2019, https://biblehub.com/text/1_peter/2-25.htm.
3. NT: 3341, Joseph Henry Thayer, *Thayer's Greek Lexicon.*
4. OT: 4496, Joseph Henry Thayer, Francis Brown, Samuel Rolles Driver, and Charles Augustus Briggs, *The Online Bible Thayer's Greek Lexicon and Brown Driver & Briggs Hebrew Lexicon.* Copyright ©

1993, Woodside Bible Fellowship, Ontario, Canada. Licensed from the Institute for Creation Research.

Frequently Asked Questions

1. NT: 4982, Blue Letter Bible, accessed March 27, 2019, https://www.blue letterbible.org/lang/lexicon/lexicon.cfm?Strongs=G4982&t=NKJV.

SPECIAL APPRECIATION

Special thanks and appreciation to all who have sent in their testimonies and praise reports to us. Kindly note that all testimonies are received in good faith and have been shared only with the consent of the testimony writers. Each testimony has been edited only for brevity and fluency. Names have been changed to protect the writers' privacy.

MEDICAL DISCLAIMER

This book is not meant to take the place of professional medical advice. If you or your loved one has a health concern or an existing medical condition, please do consult a qualified medical practitioner or healthcare provider. We would also advise you to ask and seek the Lord always for His wisdom and guidance regarding your specific health or medical issue, and to exercise godly wisdom in the management of your own physical, mental, and emotional well-being. Do not, on your own accord, disregard any professional medical advice or diagnosis. Please also do not take what has been shared in this book as permission or encouragement to stop taking your medication or going for medical treatment. While we make no guarantees and recognize that different individuals experience different results, we continue to stand in faith to believe and affirm God's Word and healing promises with all who believe.

EXTRA RESOURCES

To hear Joseph Prince preach on the biblical principles and truths shared in each chapter of this book, please check out the following audio messages at JosephPrince.com/eat.

CHAPTER 1: COME TO THE TABLE

1. Keys to Divine Health #3—Health and Wholeness Through the Holy Communion
2. Eat Your Way to Divine Health
3. Nothing Shall by Any Means Hurt You

CHAPTER 2: NOT ANOTHER DIET PLAN

1. The Health-Giving Power of the Holy Communion
2. The Holy Communion Brings Life in Your Darkest Hour
3. Have a Throne Attitude—Rest Until God Makes Your Enemies Your Footstool
4. Increasing Your Faith to Receive from the Lord

CHAPTER 3: NONE FEEBLE, NONE SICK

1. Supernatural Health Through the Roasted Lamb
2. Just a Groan Will Reach the Throne
3. Seeing Christ in the Passover

CHAPTER 4: FOR YOU, NOT AGAINST YOU

1. Rest and Wholeness Through Your Perfect High Priest
2. Live Life Loved by the Shepherd
3. Experience the Grace Revolution

CHAPTER 5: NO PLACE FOR FEAR

1. Live Life Loved by the Shepherd
2. Experience the Grace Revolution
3. Experiencing Love That Casts Out Fear
4. As Christ Is, So Are We in This World
5. Walk in Constant Victory over Fear
6. Experience God's Sure Kindness Toward You
7. Find Protection Under His Wings
8. Believe in a God Who Freely Gives
9. "Daddy, God!"—The Heart of the Father Revealed

CHAPTER 6: HE PAID THE BILL

1. Come As You Are and Receive Your Miracle
2. Being Christ-Occupied and Not Self-Occupied
3. The Ministry of the Holy Spirit Under the New Covenant

CHAPTER 7: REVELATION BRINGS RESULTS

1. Supernatural Health Through the Roasted Lamb
2. Eat Your Way to Divine Health—Part 2
3. Live Undefeated in Christ

CHAPTER 8: COMPLETELY COVERED, NO EXCLUSIONS

1. The Power of Right Believing
2. As Jesus Is, So Are You
3. Keys to Divine Health
4. Redeemed from the Curse of Sickness
5. Live the Let-Go Life
6. *No More Mind Games—Win over Discouragement and Depression* (book)

CHAPTER 9: DON'T GIVE UP!

1. Rest in Jesus' Faith for Miracles
2. Eat Your Way to Divine Health
3. Pursue the Healer and Be Healed
4. Judge God Faithful and Receive Your Miracle
5. Receiving Healing with Faith and Patience

CHAPTER 10: THE FIGHT TO REST

1. Change How You See and Change Your Life
2. *Spiritual Warfare* (book)

3. Under Attack? Put on the Armor of God!

4. Receiving Healing with Faith and Patience

5. A Fresh Revelation of the Communion Brings Healing

CHAPTER 11: GOD OF YOUR VALLEYS

1. Grace—The Key to Spiritual Warfare

2. Spiritual Warfare Myths and Truths #1

3. Eat Your Way to Divine Health—Part 2

4. The Holy Communion Brings Life in Your Darkest Hour

5. God Is a Gracious Rewarder

6. The Year of His Restoration

7. Restoration for Your Losses

CHAPTER 12: PURSUE THE HEALER

1. Reversing the Curse Through the Holy Communion

2. Receive Restoration as You Walk with Jesus

3. Your Every Blessing Is Found in the Person of Jesus

4. Pursue the Healer and Be Healed

5. Live Life Loved by the Shepherd

6. Shepherd and Sheep—the Secret to the Abundant Life

7. His Healing Is for the Undeserving

8. Discerning the Lord's Body Makes a Difference to Your Health

9. The Holy Communion Brings Life in Your Darkest Hour

SALVATION PRAYER

If you would like to receive all that Jesus has done for you and make Him your Lord and Savior, please pray this prayer:

Lord Jesus, thank You for loving me and dying for me on the cross. Your precious blood washes me clean of every sin. You are my Lord and my Savior, now and forever. I believe You rose from the dead and that You are alive today. Because of Your finished work, I am now a beloved child of God and heaven is my home. Thank You for giving me eternal life and filling my heart with Your peace and joy. Amen.

WE WOULD LIKE TO HEAR FROM YOU

If you have prayed the salvation prayer or if you have a testimony to share after reading this book, please send it to us via JosephPrince.com/testimony.

STAY CONNECTED
WITH JOSEPH

Connect with Joseph through these social media channels and receive daily inspirational teachings:

Facebook.com/JosephPrince
Twitter.com/JosephPrince
Youtube.com/JosephPrinceOnline
Instagram: @JosephPrince

FREE DAILY E-MAIL DEVOTIONAL

Sign up for Joseph's free daily e-mail devotional at
JosephPrince.com/meditate
and receive bite-size inspirations to help you grow in grace.

BOOKS BY
JOSEPH PRINCE

Healing Scriptures

Catch a glimpse of how deeply our Lord Jesus loves you and wants you healed and whole! As you read and meditate on these carefully selected healing scriptures, let His words bring life and health to every part of your body. Whether you are trusting the Lord for a healing breakthrough or simply desire to walk in better health, let the living and powerful Word of God encourage you, strengthen you, and put an end to your days of sickness and weakness!

Be sure to also get the abridged audio version of *Healing Scriptures* where Joseph reads selected portions for your daily meditation. Visit JosephPrince.com/healing for more information.

No More Mind Games

Are you battling overwhelming discouragement today? Feel imprisoned by depression and crippling, defeatist thoughts? Discover in *No More Mind Games* how you are not alone, not without help, and why you can come out of the valley stronger. Get practical keys to help you break free from depression and anxiety, and learn truths that will impart strength and hope to you. Come to know a Savior who is your very present help, who comes to you in the midst of your storm. The battle is the Lord's, and your victory is found in Him!

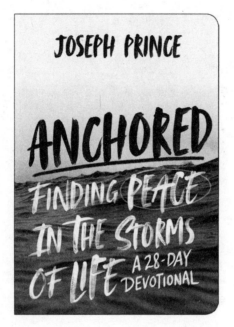

Anchored—A 28-Day Devotional

Loneliness. Inadequacy. Fear. Shame. The crushing weight of anxiety. These are storms we've all faced, storms that often threaten to engulf us. But the Lord says we can live anchored in His perfect love, grace, and righteousness through them all. Discover how in this devotional that features twenty-eight easy-to-read thoughts, weekly reflection prompts, free group-activity facilitation resources, and powerful prayer declarations. Enjoy this four-week journey on your own with the Lord, or with your family and friends! Joseph's first-ever young-adult resource will help you live anchored in Christ, no matter where you are in life.

Live the Let-Go Life

Live the Let-Go Life is the go-to resource for anyone who wants to find freedom from the stress and anxieties of modern living. Instead of letting stress and all its negative effects rule your life, discover how you can cast all your cares to the One who cares about you like no other, and experience His practical supply for every need. You'll find simple yet powerful truths and tools to help you get rid of worry and anxiety and experience greater health and well-being. Learn how you can tune in to God's peace, walk daily in His unforced rhythm of grace, and find yourself living healthier, happier, and having time for the important things in life!

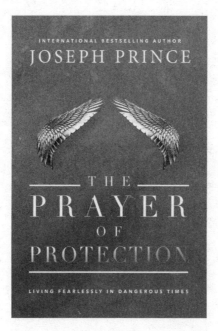

The Prayer of Protection

We live in dangerous times. A time when terrorist activities, pandemics, and natural calamities are on the rise. But there is good news. God has given us a powerful prayer of protection—Psalm 91—through which we and our families can find safety and deliverance from every snare of the enemy. In *The Prayer of Protection*, discover a God of love and His impenetrable shield of protection that covers everything that concerns you, and start living fearlessly in these dangerous times!

The Power of Right Believing

Experience transformation, breakthroughs, and freedom today through the power of right believing! This book offers seven practical and powerful keys that will help you find freedom from all fears, guilt, and addictions. See these keys come alive in the many precious testimonies you will read from people around the world who have experienced breakthroughs and liberty from all kinds of bondages. Win the battle for your mind through understanding the powerful truths of God's Word, and begin a journey of victorious living and unshakable confidence in God's love for you!

Destined to Reign

This pivotal and quintessential book on the grace of God will change your life forever! Join Joseph Prince as he unlocks foundational truths to understanding God's grace and how it alone sets you free to experience victory over every adversity, lack, and destructive habit that is limiting you today. Be uplifted and refreshed as you discover how reigning in life is all about Jesus and what He has already done for you. Start experiencing the success, wholeness, and victory that you were destined to enjoy!

ABOUT THE AUTHOR

JOSEPH **PRINCE** is a leading voice in proclaiming the gospel of grace to a whole new generation of believers and leaders. He is the senior pastor of New Creation Church in Singapore, a vibrant and dynamic church with a congregation of more than thirty-three thousand attendees. He separately heads Joseph Prince Ministries, a television and media broadcast ministry that is reaching the world with the good news about Jesus' finished work. Joseph is also the bestselling author of *The Power of Right Believing* and *Destined to Reign* and a highly sought-after conference speaker. For more information about his other inspiring resources and his latest audio and video messages, visit JosephPrince.com.